Plain English
for Lawyers

Plain English for Lawyers

FOURTH EDITION

Richard C. Wydick
PROFESSOR OF LAW
UNIVERSITY OF CALIFORNIA, DAVIS

CAROLINA ACADEMIC PRESS
Durham, North Carolina

L.C.C. No. 97-77746
ISBN: 0-89089-994-0

Carolina Academic Press
700 Kent Street
Durham, North Carolina 27701
(919) 489-7486
(919) 493-5668 FAX
www.cap-press.com
Printed in the United States

To JJW, with love

Contents

Preface and Acknowledgments

The first edition of *Plain English for Lawyers* was a revised version of an article that appeared in 66 California Law Review 727, published by the students of the University of California, Berkeley, School of Law, copyright 1978, by the California Law Review, Inc.

Many of the changes made in subsequent editions reflect the ideas, writings, and suggestions made by others who toil in the field of legal writing. My debts to them are so many that to acknowledge all of them properly in footnotes or endnotes would distract the reader—a sin that all of us in the field preach against. Thus, let me here thank my scholarly creditors in the United States, Great Britain, Canada, New Zealand, and Australia, including the following: Mark Adler, Robert Benson, Norman Brand, Robert Chaim, Robert Charrow, Veda Charrow, Martin Cutts, Robert Eagleson, J.M. Foers, Bryan A. Garner, Tom Goldstein, George Hathaway, Margaret Johns, Joseph Kimble, Jethro Lieberman, Chrissie Maher, Ray Parnas, Janice Redish, Richard Thomas, and Garth Thornton. Thanks also to Keltie Jones for her fine work on the punctuation chapter.

I owe special thanks to David Mellinkoff, Professor of Law

Emeritus at the University of California, Los Angeles. All of us in the field of legal writing have benefited from his careful scholarship and wise guidance expressed in *The Language of the Law* (1963), *Legal Writing: Sense & Nonsense* (1982), and in *Mellinkoff's Dictionary of American Legal Usage* (1992).

Richard C. Wydick
Davis, California
January 1998

Plain English
for Lawyers

Chapter 1 ——————

Why Plain English?

We lawyers do not write plain English. We use eight words to say what could be said in two. We use arcane phrases to express commonplace ideas. Seeking to be precise, we become redundant. Seeking to be cautious, we become verbose. Our sentences twist on, phrase within clause within clause, glazing the eyes and numbing the minds of our readers. The result is a writing style that has, according to one critic, four outstanding characteristics. It is "(1) wordy, (2) unclear, (3) pompous, and (4) dull."[1]

Criticism of legal writing is nothing new. In 1596, an English chancellor decided to make an example of a particularly prolix document filed in his court. The chancellor first ordered a hole cut through the center of the document, all 120 pages of it. Then he ordered that the person who wrote it should have his head stuffed through the hole, and the unfortunate fellow was led around to be exhibited to all those attending court at Westminster Hall.[2]

When the common law was transplanted to America, the writing style of the old English lawyers came with it. In 1817 Thomas Jefferson lamented that in drafting statutes his fellow lawyers were accustomed to "making every other word a 'said' or 'aforesaid' and saying everything over two or three times, so that nobody but we of the craft can untwist the diction and find out what it means...."[3]

Starting in the 1970s, criticism of legal writing took on a new intensity. The popular press castigated lawyers for the frustration and outrage that people feel when trying to puzzle through an insurance policy, an installment loan agreement, or an income tax instruction booklet. Even lawyers became critics. One lawyer charged that in writing as we do, we "unnecessarily mystify our work, baffle our clients, and alienate the public."[4]

We have made some progress during the past twenty-five years. More than a dozen good books are now available for use in law school writing courses, and most law schools now stress the need for clarity and simplicity in legal writing. In some jurisdictions, plain language is now required—or at least strongly recommended—for statutes, regulations, court rules, jury instructions, consumer contracts, insurance policies, securities disclosure documents, voter materials, and the like.[5] Lawyers who serve businesses and government agencies have learned that using plain language pays dividends: understandable warranties help sell products, and understandable government forms require less staff time to explain and reduce the number of errors made by those who fill them out.[6]

Progress, yes, but victory is not yet near. Too many law students report back from their first jobs that the clear, simple style they were urged to use in school is not acceptable to the older lawyers for whom they work. Too many jurors give up hope of comprehending the judge's instructions and rely instead on instinctive justice. Too many estate planning clients leave their lawyer's office with will and trust agreement in hand, but without fully understanding what they say. Too many people merely skim, or even ignore, the dense paragraphs of purchase agreements, apartment leases, employment contracts, and promissory notes, preferring to rely on the integrity or mercy of the author rather than to struggle with the author's legal prose.

The premise of this book is that good legal writing should not differ, without good reason, from ordinary well-written English.[7] As a well-known New York lawyer told the young associates in his firm, "Good legal writing does not sound as though it had been written by a lawyer."

In short, good legal writing is plain English. Here is an example of plain English, the statement of facts from the majority opinion in *Palsgraf v. Long Island Railroad Co.*,[8] written by Benjamin Cardozo:

> Plaintiff was standing on a platform of defendant's railroad after buying a ticket to go to Rockaway Beach. A train stopped at the station, bound for another place. Two men ran forward to catch it. One of the men reached the platform of the car without mishap, though the train was already moving. The other man, carrying a package, jumped aboard the car, but seemed unsteady as if about to fall. A guard on the car, who had held the door open, reached forward to help him in, and another guard on the platform pushed him from behind. In this act, the package was dislodged and fell upon the rails. It was a package of small size, about fifteen inches long, and was covered by newspaper. In fact it contained fireworks, but there was nothing in its appearance to give notice of its contents. The fireworks when they fell exploded. The shock of the explosion threw down some scales at the other end of the platform many feet away. The scales struck the plaintiff, causing injuries for which she sues.

What distinguishes the writing style in this passage from that found in most legal writing? Notice Justice Cardozo's economy of words. He does not say "despite the fact that the train was already moving." He says "though the train was already moving."

Notice his choice of words. He uses no archaic phrases, no misty abstractions, no hereinbefore's.

Notice his care in arranging words. There are no wide gaps

between the subjects and their verbs, nor between the verbs and their objects. There are no ambiguities to leave us wondering who did what to whom.

Notice his use of verbs. Most of them are in the simple form, and all but two are in the active voice.

Notice the length and construction of his sentences. Most of them contain only one main thought, and they vary in length: the shortest is six words, and the longest is twenty-seven words.

These and other elements of plain English style are discussed in this book. But you cannot learn to write plain English by reading a book. You must put your own pencil to paper. That is why practice exercises are included at the end of each section. When you finish the section, work the exercises. Then compare your results with those suggested in Appendix I at the end of the book. You will find additional exercises in Appendix II.

Notes

1. David Mellinkoff, The Language of the Law 23 (1963).

2. Mylward v. Welden (Ch. 1596), reprinted in C. Monro, Acta Cancellariae 692 (1847). Joseph Kimble has pointed out that the person who wrote, and subsequently wore, the offending document may have been the plaintiff's son, a non-lawyer. Professor Kimble dryly notes that the son was probably following a lawyer's form. Joseph Kimble, Plain English: A Charter for Clear Writing, 9 Cooley L. Rev. 1, n. 2 (1992), relying on Michele M. Asprey, Plain Language for Lawyers 31 (1991).

3. Letter to Joseph C. Cabell (Sept. 9, 1817), reprinted in 17 Writings of Thomas Jefferson 417–18 (A. Bergh ed. 1907).

4. Ronald Goldfarb, Lawyer Language, Litigation, Summer 1977 at 3; see also Ronald Goldfarb and James Raymond, Clear Understandings (1982).

5. See, e.g., proposed SEC regulations for securities prospectuses, 62 Fed. Reg. 3152 (1997); Bryan A. Garner, Guidelines for Drafting and Editing Court Rules, 169 F.R.D. 176 (1997); Garth C. Thornton, Legislative Drafting 46–77 (4th ed. 1996); Manual of Model Criminal Jury Instructions of the Eighth Circuit (1996); New York General Obligations Law §5-702 (McKinney Supp. 1997) (consumer contracts and leases); Florida Statutes Anno. §500.2236 (West 1996) (insurance policies). For a useful catalogue of plain English statutes, drafting manuals, jury instructions, projects, and organizations, see Joseph Kimble, Plain English: A Charter for Clear Writing, 9 Cooley L. Rev. 1, 31–58 (1992).

6. See, e.g., Gordon Mills and Mark Duckworth, The Gains from Clarity (1996) (cost-benefit study of plain language documents, sponsored by the Law Foundation of New South Wales, Australia); U.S. Dept. of Commerce, Office of Consumer Affairs, How Plain English Works for Business: Twelve Case Studies (1984).

7. This premise is taken from David Mellinkoff, The Language of the Law vii (1963); see also David Mellinkoff, Dictionary of American Legal Usage vii (1992).

8. 248 N.Y. 339, 162 N.E. 99 (1928). I have used Palsgraf as an example because it is familiar to all who have studied law. In general, however, Justice Cardozo's writing style is too ornate for modern tastes. For good examples of modern plain English style, examine the opinions of retired United States Supreme Court Justice Lewis F. Powell or United States Circuit Judge Richard Posner.

Chapter 2

Omit Surplus Words

As a beginning lawyer, I was assigned to assist an older man, a business litigator. He hated verbosity. When I would bring him what I thought was a finished piece of work, he would read it quietly and take out his pen. As I watched over his shoulder, he would strike out whole lines, turn clauses into phrases, and turn phrases into single words. One day at lunch, I asked him how he did it. He shrugged and said, "It's not hard—just omit the surplus words."

How to Spot Bad Construction

In every English sentence are two kinds of words: working words and glue words. The working words carry the meaning of the sentence. In the preceding sentence the working words are these: *working, words, carry, meaning,* and *sentence.* The others are glue words: *the, the, of,* and *the.* The glue words do perform a vital service. They hold the working words together to form a proper, grammatical sentence.[1] Without them, the sentence would read like a telegram. But if the *proportion* of glue words is too high, that is a symptom of a badly constructed sentence.

A well constructed sentence is like fine cabinetwork. The pieces are cut and shaped to fit together with scarcely any glue. When you find too many glue words in a sentence, take it apart and reshape the pieces to fit together tighter. Consider this example:

A trial by jury was requested by the defendant.

If the working words are underlined, the sentence looks like this:

A <u>trial</u> by <u>jury</u> was <u>requested</u> by the <u>defendant</u>.

Five words in that nine-word sentence are glue: *a, by, was, by,* and *the*. That proportion of glue words is too high.

How can we say the same thing in a tighter sentence with less glue? First, move *defendant* to the front and make it the subject of the sentence. Second, use *jury trial* in place of *trial by jury*. The sentence would thus read:

The defendant requested a jury trial.

If the working words are underlined, the rewritten sentence looks like this:

The <u>defendant requested</u> a <u>jury trial</u>.

Again there are four working words, but the glue words have been cut from five to two. The sentence means the same as the original, but it is tighter and one-third shorter.

Here is another example:

The ruling by the trial judge was prejudicial error for the reason that it cut off cross-examination with respect to issues that were vital.

If the working words are underlined, we have:

The <u>ruling</u> by the <u>trial judge</u> was <u>prejudicial error</u> for the <u>reason</u> that it <u>cut off cross-examination</u> with respect to <u>issues</u> that were <u>vital</u>.

In a sentence of twenty-four words, eleven carry the meaning and thirteen are glue. Again, the proportion of glue is too high.

Note the string of words, *the ruling by the trial judge*. That tells us that it was the trial judge's ruling. Why not just say *the trial judge's ruling*? The same treatment will tighten the words at the end of the sentence. *Issues that were vital* tells us that they were vital issues. Why not say *vital issues*? Now note the phrase, *for the reason that*. Does it say any more than *because*? If not, we can use one word in place of four. Likewise, *with respect to* can be reduced to *on*. Rewritten, the sentence looks like this:

The trial judge's ruling was prejudicial error because it cut off cross-examination on vital issues.

Here it is with the working words underlined:

The <u>trial judge's ruling</u> was <u>prejudicial error because</u> it <u>cut off cross-examination</u> on <u>vital issues</u>.

The revised sentence uses fifteen words in place of the original twenty-four, and eleven of the fifteen are working words. The revised sentence is both tighter and stronger than the original.

Consider a third example, but this time use a pencil and paper to rewrite the sentence yourself.

In many instances, insofar as the jurors are concerned, the jury instructions are not understandable because they are too poorly written.

Does your sentence trim the phrase *in many instances*? Here the single word *often* will suffice. Does your sentence omit the phrase *insofar as the jurors are concerned*? That adds bulk but little meaning. Finally, did you find a way to omit the clumsy *because* clause at the end of the sentence? Your rewritten sentence should look something like this:

Often jury instructions are too poorly written for the jurors to understand.

Here it is with the working words underlined:

<u>Often jury instructions are too poorly written</u> for the <u>jurors to understand.</u>

The rewritten sentence is nine words shorter than the original, and nine of its twelve words are working words.

❧ Exercise 1

Underline the working words in the sentences below. Note the proportion of glue words to working words. Then rewrite the sentences, underline the working words, and compare your results with the original sentences.

1. The testimony that was given by Reeves went to the heart of the defense that he asserted, which was his lack of the specific intent to escape.

2. In the event that there is a waiver of the attorney-client privilege by the client, the letters must be produced by the attorney for the purpose of inspection by the adversary party.

Answers on page 117. More exercises on page 133.

Avoid Compound Constructions

Compound constructions use three or four words to do the work of one or two words. They suck the vital juices from your writing. You saw some examples in the last section. *With respect to* was used instead of *on*. *For the reason that* was used instead of *because*.

Every time you see one of these pests on your page, swat it. Use a simple form instead. Here is a list of examples:

Compound	Simple
at that point in time	then
by means of	by
by reason of	because of
by virtue of	by, under
for the purpose of	to
for the reason that	because
in accordance with	by, under
inasmuch as	since
in connection with	with, about, concerning
in favor of	for
in order to	to
in relation to	about, concerning
in the event that	if
in the nature of	like
prior to	before
subsequent to	after
with a view to	to
with reference to	about, concerning

🐾 Exercise 2

Use one or two words to replace the compound constructions in these sentences.

1. The parties were in complete agreement with respect
   to the amount of rent due and also as regards the due
   date.

2. From the point of view of simplicity, an ordinary deed
   of trust would be the best.

3. On the basis of the *Burke* decision, the savings clause
   was added for the purpose of avoiding any ambiguity.

4. In terms of fairness, we should not apply the new rule
   retroactively.

5. When the funds are received, we will transfer title with
   the thought in mind of clearing up all questions as respects this matter.

6. At this point in time, I cannot recall what the letter
   was with regard to.

Answers on page 118. More exercises on page 135.

Avoid Word-Wasting Idioms

Once you develop a distaste for surplus words, you will find
many word-wasting idioms that can be trimmed from your
sentences with no loss of meaning. For instance:

The fact that the defendant was young may have influenced
the jury.

What meaning does *the fact that* add? Why not say:

The defendant's youth may have influenced the jury.

The fact that is almost always surplus. See how it can be trimmed from these examples:

Verbose	Concise
the fact that she had died	her death
he was aware of the fact that	he knew
despite the fact that	although, even though
because of the fact that	because

Likewise, words like *case, instance,* and *situation* spawn verbosity:

Verbose	Concise
in some instances the parties can	sometimes the parties can
in many cases you will find that was a situation in which the court	often you will find there the court
disability claims are now more frequent than was formerly the case	disability claims are more frequent now
injunctive relief is required in the situation in which	injunctive relief is required when
in the majority of instances the grantor will	usually the grantor will

Other examples of common word-wasting idioms that you can eliminate with no loss of meaning are:

Verbose	Concise
during the time that	during, while
for the period of	for
insofar as . . . is concerned	(omit it and start with the subject)
there is no doubt but that	doubtless, no doubt
the question as to whether	whether, the question whether
this is a topic that	this topic
until such time as	until

❧ Exercise 3

Revise these examples to omit the word-wasting idioms.

1. At such time as the judgment is entered . . .
2. This is a situation in which estoppel can be invoked . . .
3. He was sentenced to the county jail for a period of five months . . .
4. Pursuant to the terms of our contract . . .
5. There can be no doubt but that the statute applies to the situation in which . . .
6. The claim was clarified by means of a bill of particulars . . .
7. The trial judge must consider the question as to whether . . .
8. This offer will stand until such time as you . . .
9. In most instances the claimant's good faith is not disputed . . .

10. The plaintiff filed the complaint despite the fact that she knew...
11. Arbitration is useful in some instances in which the parties...
12. This is a point that has troubled many courts...
13. Because of the fact that he was injured...

Answers on page 119. More exercises on page 137.

Focus on the Actor, the Action, and the Object

One way to remedy a wordy, fogbound sentence is to ask yourself: "Who is doing what to whom in this sentence?"[2] Then rewrite the sentence to focus on those three key elements—the actor, the action, and the object of the action (if there is an object). First, state the actor. Then, state the action, using the strongest verb that will fit. Last, state the object of the action, if there is an object. Here is a simple example:

It is possible for the court to modify the judgment.

The actor is *court*, the action is *modify*, and the object of the action is *judgment*. What is the purpose of the first four words in the sentence? None. Not only are they wasted words, but they preempt the most important position in the sentence—the beginning—where the reader wants to find the actor and the action.

The sentence is both shorter and stronger when it is rewritten to focus on the actor, the action, and the object:

The court can modify the judgment.

Be alert when you find a sentence or clause that begins with *it* or *there*, followed by a form of the verb *to be*. Does the *it* or *there* refer to something specific? If not, you may be wasting words. Consider this passage:

The summons arrived this morning. It is on your desk.

The second sentence begins with *it*, followed by *is*, a form of the verb to be. The sentence is not faulty, however, because the *it* obviously refers back to *summons* in the prior sentence. But what does the *it* refer to in the following sentence?

It is obvious that the summons was not properly served.

The *it* does not refer to anything specific; rather, it points off into the fog somewhere. The sentence should be revised to read:

Obviously the summons was not properly served.

Here is a final example:

There were no reasons offered by the court for denying punitive damages.

Note that *there* is followed by *were*, a form of the verb *to be*. The *there* points off into the fog. The actor in the sentence is *court*, but it is hidden away in the middle of the sentence. The sentence would be shorter and stronger if it read:

The court offered no reasons for denying punitive damages.

❧ Exercise 4

Rewrite these sentences, omitting surplus words and focusing on the actor, the action, and the object of the action.

1. There are three misstatements of fact in appellant's opening brief.
2. It is not necessary for the witness to sign the deposition transcript until the errors are corrected.
3. In approving a class action settlement, it is imperative for the court to guard the interests of class members who are not present.
4. There is nothing to tell us whether this misconduct on the part of trial counsel influenced the jury's verdict.
5. It has been nine weeks since we served our first set of interrogatories.

Answers on page 119. More exercises on page 139.

Do Not Use Redundant Legal Phrases

Why do lawyers use the term *null and void*? According to the dictionary, either *null* or *void* by itself would do the job. But the lawyer's pen seems impelled to write *null and void*, as though driven by primordial instinct. An occasional lawyer, perhaps believing that *null and void* looks naked by itself, will write *totally null and void*, or perhaps *totally null and void and of no further force or effect whatsoever*.

The phrase *null and void* is an example of coupled synonyms—a pair or string of words with the same or nearly the same meaning.[3] Here are other common examples:

alter or change	last will and testament
confessed and acknowledged	made and entered into
convey, transfer, and set over	order and direct
for and during the period	peace and quiet
force and effect	rest, residue, and remainder
free and clear	save and except
full and complete	suffer or permit
give, devise and bequeath	true and correct
good and sufficient	undertake and agree

Coupled synonyms have ancient roots. Professor Mellinkoff explains[4] that, at several points in history, the English and their lawyers had two languages to choose from: first, a choice between the language of the Celts and that of their Anglo-Saxon conquerors; later, a choice between English and Latin; and later still, a choice between English and French. Lawyers started using a word from each language, joined in a pair, to express a single meaning. (For example, *free and clear* comes from the Old English *freo* and the Old French *cler*.) This redundant doubling was sometimes used for clarity, sometimes for emphasis, and sometimes just because it was the literary fashion. Doubling became traditional in legal language, and it persisted long after any practical purpose was dead.

Ask a modern lawyer why he or she uses a term like *suffer or permit* in a simple apartment lease. The first answer will likely be: "for precision." True, *suffer* has a slightly different meaning than its companion *permit*. But *suffer* in this sense is now rare in ordinary usage, and *permit* would do the job if it were used alone.

The lawyer might then tell you that *suffer or permit* is better because it is a traditional legal term of art. Traditional it may be, but a term of art it is not. A term of art is a short expression that (a) conveys a fairly well-agreed meaning, and (b) saves the many words that would otherwise be needed to convey that meaning. *Suffer or permit* fails to satisfy the second condition, and perhaps the first as well.

The word *hearsay* is an example of a true term of art. First, its core meaning is fairly well agreed in modern evidence law, although its meaning at the margin has always inspired scholarly debate.[5] Second, *hearsay* enables a lawyer to use one word instead of many to say that a statement is being offered into evidence to prove that what it asserts is true, and that the statement is not one made by the declarant while testifying at the trial or hearing. One word that can say all that deserves our praise and deference. But *suffer or permit* does not.

Suffer or permit probably found its way into that apartment lease because the lawyer was working from a form that had been used around the office for years. The author of the form, perhaps long dead, probably worked from some even older form that might, in turn, have been inspired by a formbook or some now defunct appellate case where the phrase was used but not examined.

If you want your writing to have a musty, formbook smell, by all means use as many coupled synonyms as you can find. If you want it to be crisp, do not use any.[6] When one looms up on your page, stop to see if one of the several words, or perhaps a fresh word, will carry your intended meaning. You will find, for example, that the phrase *last will and testament* can be replaced by the single word *will*.[7]

This is not as simple as it sounds. Lawyers are busy, cautious people, and they cannot afford to make mistakes. The old, redundant phrase has worked in the past; a new one may somehow raise a question. To check it in the law library will take time, and time is the lawyer's most precious commodity. But remember—once you slay one of these old monsters, it will stay dead for the rest of your legal career. If your memory is short, keep a card or computer file of slain redundancies. Such trophies distinguish a lawyer from a scrivener.

❧ Exercise 5

In the following passage you will find all the kinds of surplus words discussed in chapter 2. Rewrite the passage, omitting as many surplus words as you can.

> We turn now to the request which has been made by the plaintiff for the issuance of injunctive relief. With respect to this request, the argument has been made by the defendant that injunctive relief is not necessary because of the fact that the exclusionary clause is already null and void by reason of the prior order and decree of this court. This being the case, the exclusionary clause can have no further force or effect, and the defendant argues that in such an instance full and complete relief can be given without the issuance of an injunction. There is obvious merit in defendant's contention, and it is for that reason that we have reached a decision not to grant injunctive relief herein.

Answer on page 120. Additional exercise on page 140.

Notes

1. Robert Chaim has pointed out that my distinction between glue words and working words is roughly similar to a more precise classification used by some grammarians. See Robert A. Chaim, A Model for the Analysis of the Language of Lawyers, 33 J. Legal Educ. 120, n.31 (1983). Dean Chaim refers to the writings of Randolph Quirk and Quirk's co-authors, who divide the parts of speech

into "closed classes" and "open classes." The closed classes (roughly similar to my glue word category) include prepositions, pronouns, articles, demonstratives, conjunctions, modal verbs (such as *can, must, will,* and *could*), and primary verbs (such as *be, have,* and *do*). The closed classes contain a relatively small number of words, and they cannot normally be extended by the addition of new words. The words in a closed class are "mutually exclusive," meaning that the decision to use one of them precludes using a different one. (If *on* expresses the intended meaning, then *below* cannot be substituted for it.) Further, the words in a closed class are "mutually defining," meaning that it is harder to define an individual item than to define it in relation to the rest of the class. In contrast, the open classes (roughly similar to my working word category) include nouns, full verbs (such as *steal, bake,* and *haggle*), adjectives, and adverbs. The open classes are indefinitely extendable. New words are constantly being added, and no inventory of nouns, for example, could ever be complete. See Randolph Quirk, Sidney Greenbaum, Geoffrey Leech, and Jan Svartvik, A Comprehensive Grammar of the English Language 67–75 (1985).

2. This prescription is part of a "Paramedic Method" devised by Professor Richard A. Lanham for rendering first aid to sick sentences. See Richard A. Lanham, Revising Prose 1–9 (2d ed. 1987). See also Joseph M. Williams, Style: Ten Lessons in Clarity and Grace (5th ed. 1997).

3. See David Mellinkoff, Dictionary of American Legal Usage 129–32 (1992); see also Mark Duckworth and Arthur Spyrou, Law Words: Thirty Essays on Legal Words and Phrases (Centre for Plain Legal Language, University of Sydney, Australia 1995).

4. David Mellinkoff, The Language of the Law (1963) 38–39, 121–22.

5. See Fed. R. Evid. 801(c); Charles T. McCormick, McCormick on Evidence §§246–51 (John W. Strong gen. ed., 4th ed. 1992).

6. Professor Mellinkoff notes that a few coupled synonyms have become so "welded by usage" that they act as a single term. These

can be tolerated when used in their proper legal context. His examples include the following: *aid and abet, aid and comfort, cease and desist, full faith and credit, metes and bounds,* and *pain and suffering.* David Mellinkoff, Dictionary of American Legal Usage 129–32 (1992); but see Bryan A. Garner, A Dictionary of Modern Legal Usage 292–95 (2d ed. 1995).

7. Mellinkoff, supra note 6 at 686–87.

Chapter 3

Use Base Verbs, Not Nominalizations

At its core, the law is not abstract. It is part of a real world full of people who live and move and do things to other people. Car drivers *collide*. Plaintiffs *complain*. Judges *decide*. Defendants *pay*.

To express this life and motion, a writer must use verbs—action words. The purest verb form is the base verb, like *collide, complain, decide,* and *pay.* Base verbs are simple creatures. They cannot tolerate adornment. If you try to dress them up, you squash their life and motion. The base verb *collide* can be decked out as a noun, *collision*. Likewise, *complain* becomes *complaint. Decide* becomes *decision. Pay* becomes *payment.*

A base verb that has been turned into a noun is called a "nominalization." Lawyers and bureaucrats love nominalizations. Lawyers and bureaucrats do not *act*—they *take action.* They do not *assume*—they *make assumptions.* They do not *conclude*—they *draw conclusions.*

If you use nominalizations instead of base verbs, surplus words begin to swarm like gnats. "Please *state* why you *object* to the question," comes out like this: "Please *make a statement* of why you are *interposing an objection* to the question." The base verb *state* can do the work all alone. But to get the same work out of *statement*, you need a supporting verb (*make*), an article (*a*), and a preposition (*of*). The word *objection* attracts a similar cloud of surplus words.

You can spot most of the common nominalizations by their endings:

-al	-ment	-ant
-ence	-ion	-ent
-ancy	-ency	-ance
-ity		

Not all words with those endings are nominalizations. Further, not all nominalizations are bad. Sometimes you cannot avoid them. But do not overuse them; when you find one on your page, stop to see if you can make your sentence shorter and stronger by using a base verb instead.

🐾 Exercise 6

Rewrite these sentences omitting surplus words and using base verbs in place of nominalizations.

1. Section 1038 has pertinence to any contract that makes provision for attorney fees.
2. Commencement of discovery is not dependent on the judge's consideration of the motion.
3. We are in agreement with your position, but if it is your intention to cause delay, we will stand in opposition to you.

4. The effectuation of improvement in downstream water quality has as a requirement our termination of the pollution of the headwaters.

5. If there is a continuation of this breach, my client will effect an immediate termination of the contract.

6. Amendment of the interrogatory answer is clearly proper, but if we make an amendment at this point in time, the court may have some suspicion with respect to our client's good faith.

7. Fulfillment of the testator's wishes is an impossibility unless this court orders an invalidation of the inter vivos transfer.

8. Cooperation with you is our sincere desire, and we hope you are willing to undertake serious reconsideration of your position. Your refusal to do so, and your failure to accomplish the completion of the work on schedule, would cause us to commence impoundment of your funds.

Answers on page 120. More exercises on page 141.

Chapter 4 —————————————————————————

Prefer the Active Voice

The Difference Between Active and Passive Voice

When you use a verb in the active voice, the subject of the sentence does the acting. "John kicks the ball," is in the active voice. *John* is the subject, and John does the acting: he kicks the ball. When you use a verb in the passive voice, the subject of the sentence is acted upon. "The ball is kicked by John," is in the passive voice. *Ball* is the subject, and the ball is being acted upon: it is kicked by John.

Active
John kicked the ball.

Passive
The ball was kicked by John.

The two sentences mean the same thing, but observe that the sentence in the passive voice is longer than the sentence in the active voice. In the active voice, the single word *kicks* expresses the action all by itself. The passive voice needs three words, *is kicked by*, to express the same action. Thus, one good reason to prefer the active voice is economy—the active voice takes fewer words. Notice that in each of the following examples, the active voice takes fewer words than the passive voice:

Active	Passive
The union filed a complaint.	A complaint was filed by the union.
The trial judge will deny your motion.	Your motion will be denied by the trial judge.
The legislative history supports our conclusion.	Our conclusion is supported by the legislative history.
The trustor had not intended the trust to...	The trust had not been intended by the trustor to...

Both the active voice and the passive voice can express action in various tenses, that is, action at various times. For example:

Active	Passive
John kicked the ball.	The ball was kicked by John.
John kicks the ball.	The ball is kicked by John.
John will kick the ball.	The ball will be kicked by John.
John has kicked the ball.	The ball has been kicked by John.
John had kicked the ball.	The ball had been kicked by John.
John will have kicked the ball.	The ball will have been kicked by John.

No matter what the verb tense—past, present, future, or something more complicated—the key difference between the active and passive voice remains the same: in the active voice, the subject of the sentence does the acting, but in the passive voice, the subject of the sentence is acted upon.

✿ Exercise 7

First, underline the verbs in these sentences. (Note that some of the sentences have more than one verb.) Then identify each verb as either active voice or passive voice.

1. The admissibility of post-hypnotic testimony was questioned by the Fourth Circuit in the *Forbush* case.
2. The prosecutor has petitioned for certiorari, but the petition will probably be denied by the Supreme Court.
3. If certiorari had been granted by the Supreme Court in one of the earlier cases, we would not now face a split among the circuits.
4. The split among the circuits has existed for nearly a decade.
5. The liberal approach, which the Ninth Circuit pioneered eight years ago, has been rejected in the Second and Fifth Circuits.
6. The conservative approach suggests that in *Forbush* the testimony should not have been admitted by the trial court.

Answers on page 121. More exercises on page 142.

The Passive Can Create Ambiguity

The passive voice takes more words than the active voice, but that is not its only disadvantage. The passive voice can be ambiguous. With the active voice, you can usually tell who is doing what to whom. With the passive voice, however, the writer can hide the identity of the actor. That construction is called the "truncated passive." For example: "The ball was kicked." Who kicked the ball? We have no way to know; the actor is hidden in the fog of the truncated passive. Bureaucrats love to write in the truncated passive because it lets them hide in the fog; the reader cannot discover who is responsible for the action (or the lack of it). A writer who wants to befog the matter totally will couple the truncated passive with a nominalization, like this: "A kicking action was accomplished," thus hiding both the kicker and the kickee.

The truncated passive can be especially troublesome in legal writing. Consider this patent license provision:

> All improvements of the patented invention that are made hereafter shall promptly be disclosed, and failure to do so shall be deemed a material breach of this license agreement.

Who must disclose improvements to whom? Must the licensor disclose improvements it makes to the licensee? Must the licensee disclose improvements it makes to the licensor? Must each party disclose improvements it makes to the other party? If it ever becomes important to know, the parties will probably have to slug it out in a lawsuit, all because of the truncated passive voice.

Notice that the title of this chapter says *prefer* the active voice. It does not say never use the passive voice. The passive voice has its proper uses. First, you can use it when the thing done is important, and who did it is not:

The subpoena was served on January 19th.

Second, you can use it when you don't know who did it:

The ledgers were mysteriously destroyed.

Third, you can use it to place a strong element at the end of the sentence for emphasis:

When he walked through the door, the victim was shot.

Fourth, you can use it when a sense of detached abstraction is appropriate:

In the eyes of the law, all persons are created equal.

Fifth, you can use it when you want to muddy the waters. For example, if you do not want to state outright that your client knocked out the plaintiff's teeth, you can say:

The plaintiff's teeth were knocked out.

Thus, if you can articulate a sound reason for using the passive voice, then use it. But elsewhere, use the active voice; it will make your writing clearer and more concise.

❧ Exercise 8

Rewrite these sentences, omitting surplus words and using the active voice unless you can articulate a good reason for using the passive voice. Supply any missing information that you need.

1. Clients' funds that have been received by an attorney must be put into the Client Trust Account.

2. This agreement may be terminated by either party by thirty days' notice being given to the other party.

3. Each month price lists were exchanged between the defendant manufacturers, and it was agreed that all sales would be made at list prices or above.

4. If I am not survived by my husband by thirty days, my children are to receive such of those items of my personal property as may be selected for them by my executor.

5. It was insisted by the supplier that the goods were of merchantable quality.

6. In certain instances, a Form 242A request must be received and approved before customs clearance will be granted. No action will be taken with respect to customs clearance until the Form 242A request has been acted upon favorably. Where it is determined that no Form 242A request need be filed, steps may be taken to effect customs clearance without delay.

Answers on page 121. More exercises on page 143.

Use Short Sentences

For centuries, English-speaking lawyers have been addicted to long, complicated sentences. The long sentence habit began back when English writers used punctuation to guide oral delivery, rather than to convey meaning.[1] In law, the long sentence habit persisted even after orderly division of thought had become routine in ordinary English prose. When lawyers write, they deliver to the reader in one gigantic package all their main themes, supporting reasons, details, qualifications, exceptions, and conclusions. In particular, statutes and regulations grind on, line after line, perhaps on the theory that if the readers come to a period they will rush out to violate the law without bothering to read to the end. Consider this criminal statute:

Any person who, by means of any machine, instrument, or contrivance, or in any other manner, intentionally taps, or makes any unauthorized connection, whether physically, electrically, acoustically, inductively, or otherwise, with any telegraph or telephone wire, line, cable, or instrument of any internal telephonic communications system, or who willfully and without consent of all parties to the communication, or in an unauthorized manner, reads, or attempts to read, or to learn the contents or meaning of any message, report, or communication while the same is in transit or passing over any wire, line or cable, or is being sent from or received at any place within this state; or who uses, or attempts to use, in any manner, or for any purpose, or to communicate in any way, any information so obtained, or who aids, agrees with, employs, or conspires with any person or persons to unlawfully do, or permit, or cause to be done any of the acts or things mentioned above in this section, is punishable by a fine not exceeding two thousand five hundred dollars ($2,500), or by imprisonment in the county jail not exceeding one year, or by imprisonment in the state prison not exceeding three years, or by both such fine and imprisonment in the county jail or in the state prison.[2]

That sentence contains 242 words and no fewer than eighteen separate thoughts. No wonder it is hard to swallow.

Long sentences make legal writing hard to understand. To prove this to yourself, read the following passage at your normal speed. Then ask yourself what it means.

In a trial by jury, the court may, when the convenience of witnesses or the ends of justice would be promoted thereby, on motion of a party, after notice and hearing, make an order, no later than the close of the pretrial conference in cases in which such pretrial conference is to be held, or in other cases, no later than 10 days before the trial date, that the trial of the issue of liability shall precede the trial of any other issue in the case.

The subject matter of that passage is not profound or complicated, but the passage is hard to understand. It consists of a single sentence, eighty-six words long, containing five pieces of information:

1. In a jury case, the liability issue may be tried before any other issue.
2. The judge may order the liability issue to be tried first if that will serve the convenience of witnesses or the ends of justice.

3. The judge may make the order on a party's motion, after notice and hearing.

4. In a case with a pretrial conference, the judge may make the order no later than the end of the conference.

5. In a case with no pretrial conference, the judge may make the order no later than ten days before the trial date.

The original passage is hard to understand for two reasons. First, the single-sentence format caused the author to distort the logical order of the five pieces of information. The first thing the readers want to know is what the passage is about. It is about the trial of the liability issue before other issues. But before the readers discover that, they must climb through a thicket of subsidiary ideas and arrive at the last twenty words of the sentence.

Second, the single-sentence format strains a reader's memory. The subject of the sentence (*court*) appears at word seven. At word thirty-two, the verb (*make*) finally shows up. Part of the object (*an order*) comes next, but the critical part remains hidden until the reader arrives, breathless, at word sixty-eight. By then the reader has forgotten the subject and verb and must search back in the sentence to find them.

The remedy for such a passage is simple. Instead of one long sentence containing five thoughts, use five sentences, each containing one thought. Here is one way the passage could be rewritten:

In a jury case, the court may order the liability issue to be tried before any other issue. The court may make such an order if doing so serves the convenience of witnesses or the ends of justice. The court may make the order on a party's motion, after notice and hearing. In a case with a pretrial conference, the court may make the order no later than the end of the conference. In a case with no pretrial conference, the court may make the order no later than ten days before the trial date.

Instead of one eighty-seven word sentence, we now have five sentences with an average length of eighteen words. Each sentence contains only one main thought, and the thoughts follow in logical sequence.

Passages like the one above suggest a two-part guide to clarity and ease of understanding in legal writing:

1. In *most* sentences, put only one main thought.
2. Keep the *average* sentence length below twenty-five words.[3]

Do not misinterpret this guide. Part 1 says that *most* sentences should contain only one main thought. It does *not* say that *every* sentence should contain only one main thought. To keep the reader's interest, you need variety in sentence construction: some simple sentences that express only one main thought, interspersed with some compound or complex sentences that express two or more related thoughts.

Likewise, Part 2 says that the *average* length of your sentences should be below twenty-five words. It does *not* say that *every* sentence should be twenty-five words or less. You need variety in sentence length as well as sentence construction: some short sentences, some of medium length, and an occasional long one in which related thoughts are joined.

When you write a long sentence, however, bear in mind Mark Twain's advice. After recommending short sentences as the general rule, he added:

At times [the writer] may indulge himself with a long one, but he will make sure there are no folds in it, no vaguenesses, no parenthetical interruptions of its view as a whole;

when he has done with it, it won't be a sea-serpent with half of its arches under the water; it will be a torch-light procession.[4]

&. Exercise 9

Rewrite these passages using short sentences and omitting as many surplus words as you can.

1. By establishing a technique whereby the claims of many individuals can be resolved at the same time, class actions serve an important function in our judicial system in eliminating the possibility of repetitious litigation and providing claimants with a method of obtaining enforcement of claims that would otherwise be too small to warrant individual litigation.

2. While there are instances in which consumer abuse and exploitation result from advertising that is false, misleading, or irrelevant, it does not necessarily follow that these cases need to be remedied by governmental intervention in the marketplace because it is possible for consumers' interests to be protected through resort to the courts, either by consumers themselves or by those competing sellers who see their market shares decline in the face of inroads based on such advertising.

3. Absent from the majority opinion is any consideration of the fact that the individual states, both as a matter of common law and additionally as a matter of federal constitutional law, have traditionally been regarded as sovereigns, in consequence of which legal

doctrines such as laches, acquiescence, estoppel, as well as stat-utes of limitations of the type at issue in the present litigation, are not generally applied to claims made by states.

Answers on page 122. More exercises on page 146.

Notes

1. The history of the long, long sentence is told in David Mellinkoff, The Language of the Law 152–70 (1963); see also David Mellinkoff, Legal Writing: Sense & Nonsense 58–60 (1982).

2. Cal. Pen. Code §631(a) (West 1997 Supp.).

3. To measure sentence length, pick a paragraph or two and count the number of words from one period to the next. Count hyphenated words and groups of symbols as one word. Do not count legal citations. For example, this sentence would be counted as 20 words:

```
  1        2         3      4       5     6     7
The twin-drive concept was obvious from IBM's

  8    9      10    11     12     13
'497 patent; under the Graham test, 382 U.S.

              14   15   16   17    18      19   20
at 17-18, that is enough to invalidate Claim 12.
```

When you measure a tabulated sentence (see page 47), regard the initial colon and the semicolons as periods. For other views about the importance of sentence length, see generally Theodore M. Bernstein, Watch Your Language 111–21 (Atheneum 1983); Fry, A Readability Formula that Saves Time, 11 Journal of Reading 513 (1968). For a more complicated readability formula, see Rudolf Flesch, How to Write Plain English: A Book for Lawyers & Consumers 20–32 (1979).

4. As quoted in Ernest Gowers, The Complete Plain Words 166–67 (1st U.S. ed., revised by Sidney Greenbaum and Janet Whitcut, 1988).

Chapter 6 ——————————————————————

Arrange Your Words with Care

Avoid Wide Gaps Between the Subject, the Verb, and the Object

To make your writing easy to understand, most of your sentences should follow the normal English word order: first the subject, next the verb, and then the object (if there is one). For example:

       subject   verb
The <u>defendant</u> <u>demurred</u>.

       subject   verb   object
The <u>defendant</u> <u>filed</u> six <u>affidavits</u>.

In seeking to understand a sentence, the reader's mind searches for the subject, the verb, and the object. If those three key elements are set out in that order and close together in the sentence, then the reader will understand quickly.

Lawyers, however, like to test the agility of their readers by making them leap wide gaps between the subject and the verb and between the verb and the object. For example:

> A claim, which in the case of negligent misconduct shall not exceed $500, and in the case of intentional misconduct shall not exceed $1,000, may be filed with the Office of the Administrator by any injured party.

In that sentence, the reader must leap a twenty-two word gap to get from the subject (claim) to the verb (may be filed). The best remedy for a gap that wide is to turn the intervening words into a separate sentence:

> Any injured party may file a claim with the Office of the Administrator. A claim must not exceed $500 for negligent misconduct, or $1,000 for intentional misconduct.

Smaller gaps between subject and verb can be closed by moving the intervening words to the beginning or the end of the sentence:

Gap	Gap Closed
This agreement, unless revocation has occurred at an earlier date, shall expire on November 1, 2006.	Unless sooner revoked, this agreement expires on November 1, 2006.
The defendant, in addition to having to pay punitive damages, may be liable for plaintiff's costs and attorney fees.	The defendant may have to pay plaintiff's costs and attorney fees in addition to punitive damages.

The problem is the same when the gap comes between the verb and the object:

The proposed statute gives to any person who suffers financial injury by reason of discrimination based on race, religion, sex, or physical handicap a cause of action for treble damages.

Here a twenty-one word gap comes between the verb (gives) and the direct object (cause of action). One remedy is to make two sentences. Another is to move the intervening words to the end of the sentence:

The proposed statute gives a cause of action for treble damages to any person who suffers financial injury because of discrimination based on race, religion, sex, or physical handicap.

🏵 Exercise 10

Close the gaps in each sentence by moving the intervening words or by splitting the sentence in two. When you rewrite, omit surplus words.

1. A response must, within twenty days after service of the petition has been made, be filed with the hearing officer.

2. The attorney-client privilege, while applying to the client's revelation of a past crime, has no application when the client seeks the aid of the attorney with respect to the planning or carrying out of a future crime.

3. The sole eyewitness, having seen the accident from the window of an apartment that was on the seventh floor of a building located one-half block in a northerly di-

rection from the intersection, testified that she did not see which car made the first entry into the intersection.

4. Jose Cruz, who was the plaintiff's grandfather, later transferred, by a deed of gift that was bitterly contested by the heirs but that was ultimately upheld by the probate court, the 200 acres that are now in dispute.

Answers on page 123. More exercises on page 148.

Put Conditions and Exceptions Where They Are Clear and Easy to Read

When lawyers draft contracts, statutes, rules, and the like, they often use conditions (if A and B, then C) and exceptions (D, except when E or F). One can imagine a language with strict rules about where in a sentence to put conditions and exceptions—for example, a rule that conditions always go at the beginning of the sentence and exceptions always go at the end. The English language has no such rules, so one must decide, sentence by sentence, where to put conditions and exceptions, guided by the need for clarity and readability.[1] Usually, the *end* of the sentence is the best place for a condition or exception that is longer than the main clause. For example:

> A lawyer may disclose a client's confidential information *if disclosure is necessary to prevent the client from committing a crime that will cause death or substantial bodily injury.*

Conversely, the *beginning* of the sentence is usually the best place if the condition or exception is short, or if it needs to be at the beginning to avoid leading the reader astray. For example:

Except for U.S. citizens, all persons passing this point must have in their possession a valid passport, a baggage clearance certificate, and a yellow entry card.

When Necessary, Tabulate

Sometimes the best way to present a cluster of conditions, or exceptions, or other closely related ideas is in one long sentence, split up like a laundry list. This device is called "tabulation."[2] Here is a sentence that could benefit from tabulation:

You can qualify for benefits under Section 43 if you are sixty-four or older and unable to work, and that section also provides benefits in the event that you are blind in one eye, or both eyes, or are permanently disabled in the course of your employment.

When tabulated, the sentence looks like this:

You can qualify for benefits under Section 43 if you meet any one of the following conditions:
- you are 64 or older and are unable to work; or
- you are blind in one or both eyes; or
- you are permanently disabled in the course of your employment.

When you tabulate, follow these conventions:

1. Each item in the list must be of the same class. Don't make a list like this:
   a. bread;
   b. eggs; and
   c. Czar Nicholas II.

2. Each item in the list must fit, in substance and grammar, with the material in front of the colon and the material following the list. Don't make a list like this:

   a. jurisdiction;
   b. venue; and
   c. preparing charts for Dr. Sullivan's testimony.

3. After each item in the list, except the last, put a semicolon followed by *or* (if the list is disjunctive) or *and* (if the list is conjunctive). If both the list and the items are short, and if the reader will not become confused, you can omit the *and* or *or* after all except the next-to-last item.

As shown above, tabulation can also be used to bring order to a series of related, complete sentences.

❧ Exercise 11

Use tabulation to clarify this passage.

Venue would be proper, unless the claim is framed as a federal question, in the Southern District of New York, if that is where the plaintiff resides, or in the Eastern District of California, assuming that the defendant does business in that judicial district, or in the Northern District of Illinois, if that turns out to be the place where the events in question happened.

Answer on page 123. More exercises on page 150.

Put Modifying Words Close to What They Modify

In some languages, the order of words within a sentence does not affect the meaning of the sentence. But in English, word order does affect meaning, as this sentence shows:

The defendant was arrested for fornicating under a little-used state statute.

Modifying words tend to do their work on whatever you put them near. Therefore, as a general rule, put modifying words as close as you can to the words you want them to modify. That will help avoid sentences like these:

My client has discussed your proposal to fill the drainage ditch with his partners.

Being beyond any doubt insane, Judge Weldon ordered the petitioner's transfer to a state mental hospital.

Beware of the "squinting" modifier—one that sits mid-sentence and can be read to modify either what precedes it or what follows it:

A trustee who steals dividends often cannot be punished.

What does *often* modify? Does the sentence tell us that crime frequently pays? Or that frequent crime pays?

Once discovered, a squinting modifier is easy to cure. Either choose a word that does not squint, or rearrange the sentence to avoid the ambiguity. For example:

When workers are injured frequently no compensation is paid.

If that means that injured workers frequently receive no compensation, the squinting modifier could be moved to the front of the sentence, like this:

Frequently, workers who are injured receive no compensation.

The word *only* is a notorious troublemaker. For example, in the following sentence the word *only* could go in any of seven places and produce a half a dozen different meanings:

She said that he shot her.

To keep *only* under control, put it immediately before the word you want it to modify. If it creates ambiguity in that position, try to isolate it at the beginning or ending of the sentence:

Ambiguous	**Clear**
Lessee shall use the vessel only for recreation.	Lessee must use the vessel for recreation only.
Shares are sold to the public only by the parent corporation.	Only the parent corporation sells shares to the public.

Watch out for ambiguity in sentences like this one:

The grantor was Maxwell Aaron, the father of Sarah Aaron, who later married Pat Snyder.

Who married Pat—Maxwell or Sarah? Some lawyers try to clear up this kind of ambiguity by piling on more words:

The grantor was Maxwell Aaron, father of Sarah Aaron, which said Maxwell Aaron later married Pat Snyder.

But it's easier than that. You can usually avoid ambiguity by placing the relative pronoun (like *who*, *which*, and *that*) right after the word to which it relates. If Pat's spouse were Maxwell, the sentence could be rearranged to read:

> The grantor was Sarah Aaron's father, Maxwell Aaron, who later married Pat Snyder.

Sometimes a relative pronoun will not behave, no matter where you put it:

> Claims for expenses, which must not exceed $100, must be made within 30 days.

What must not exceed $100—the claims or the expenses? Here the best remedy is simply to omit the relative pronoun:

> Claims for expenses must not exceed $100 and must be made within 30 days.

or

> Expenses must not exceed $100. Claims for expenses must be made within 30 days.

❧ Exercise 12

Rewrite these sentences to solve the modifier problems. If a sentence has more than one possible meaning, select whichever one you wish and rewrite the sentence to express that meaning unambiguously.

1. The plaintiff's pain can be alleviated only by expensive therapy.

2. Being ignorant of the law, the attorney argued that his client should receive a light sentence.

3. Defendant's argument overlooks an amendment to the statute that was enacted in 1994.

4. Under Section 309, attorney fees only can be awarded when the claim is brought without good faith.

5. Apparently this special tax provision was intended to encourage the production of cotton in the eyes of Congress.

Answers on page 124. More exercises on page 151.

Avoid Nested Modifiers

When I was a child, one of my favorite toys was a figure carved from smooth dark wood, the figure of a seated, round Navajo woman. She came apart in the middle to reveal an identical but smaller woman inside. The second woman likewise came apart to reveal a third, and the third a fourth.

Perverse lawyers write sentences that are constructed like my Navajo women. For example:

Defendant, who was driving a flatbed truck that was laden with a tangle of old furniture some of which was not tied down securely, stopped without warning.

Here is the same sentence written with brackets and parentheses:

Defendant {who was driving a flatbed truck [that was laden with a tangle of old furniture (some of which was not tied down securely)]} stopped without warning.

That sentence is like my Navajo women because it contains a set of modifying phrases, each nested inside the next. The sentence is hard to understand because the reader must mentally supply brackets and parentheses to keep the modifiers straight.

The best remedy for such a sentence is to take apart the nest of modifiers and put some of the information in a separate sentence. Consider this passage for example:

> A claim for exemption, which in the case of a dwelling that is used for housing not more than a single family shall not exceed $30,000 or the fair market value, whichever is less, may be filed with the Administrator within 90 days after receipt of notice.

When broken in two, the passage reads like this:

> A claim for exemption may be filed with the Administrator within 90 days after receipt of notice. The claim for a single family dwelling cannot exceed $30,000, or the fair market value, whichever is less.

❧ Exercise 13

Rewrite these sentences without the nested modifiers. As you rewrite, omit surplus words.

1. Appellant which was represented in this case by the firm of Bishop & Donald, counsel of long experience in government contract litigation, a field that requires no small degree of expertise, must have recognized the weakness of its claim.

2. The proposed legal ethics rule would require an attorney to place all funds received on behalf of a client, including an advance for attorney fees not yet earned, but not including a flat fee paid in advance, in the attorney's client trust fund account.

Answers on page 124. More exercises on page 152.

Clarify the Reach of Modifiers

Suppose that the owner of a pet store agrees to sell part of her stock to someone else. The contract of sale states that it covers "all female rabbits and hamsters over six weeks old." The contract is ambiguous, and the ambiguity is caused by the uncertain reach of the two modifiers *female* and *over six weeks old*.[3] We can't tell whether *female* stops with *rabbits*, or whether it reaches forward to *hamsters* as well. Further, we can't tell whether *over six weeks old* stops with *hamsters*, or whether it reaches backward to *rabbits* as well. Thus, the contract may cover any of four combinations:

1. [all female rabbits, however old] + [all hamsters over six weeks old, of whatever sex]; or

2. [all female rabbits, however old] + [all female hamsters over six weeks old]; or

3. [all female rabbits over six weeks old] + [all hamsters over six weeks old, of whatever sex]; or

4. [all female rabbits over six weeks old] + [all female hamsters over six weeks old].

To avoid this kind of ambiguity, you must clarify the reach of the modifiers in your sentences. Sometimes you can do that simply by changing the word order:

Ambiguous	Clear
women and men over 30	men over 30 and women
rental payments and fees from licensees	fees from licensees and rental payments

Other times, you can clarify the reach of a modifier by repeating a few words, or making a list, or tabulating.

Ambiguous	Clear
endangered frogs and salamanders	endangered frogs and endangered salamanders
all vans, sport vehicles, autos, and trucks without four-wheel drive	all vehicles without four-wheel drive, including vans, sport vehicles, autos, and trucks

Exercise 14

Clarify the reach of the modifiers in these sentences. If a sentence has more than one possible meaning, select whichever one you wish and revise the sentence to express that meaning unambiguously.

1. The freshwater vessel tax must be paid on all sailboats and inboard motor boats over 18 feet in length.

2. Professional discipline can be imposed if an attorney is convicted of a felony or misdemeanor that involves moral turpitude.

3. Under the state's hearsay rule, "former testimony" means testimony taken at an earlier hearing or deposi-

tion in the same or a different case, or in any other formal adjudicative proceeding conducted by a governmental agency, provided that the testimony is taken under oath.

Answers on page 124. More exercises on page 153.

Notes

1. For more specific guidance, see Bryan A. Garner, Guidelines for Drafting and Editing Court Rules, 169 F.R.D. 177, 190–94 (1997).

2. See Reed Dickerson, The Fundamentals of Legal Drafting 115–24 (2d ed. 1986).

3. Id. at 101–114; G.C. Thornton, Legislative Drafting 22–28 (4th ed. 1996); Veda Charrow, Myra Erhardt & Robert Charrow, Clear and Effective Legal Writing 170–72 (2d ed. 1995).

Chapter 7

Choose Your Words with Care

Here are two ways a lawyer might begin a letter to a client to explain why the lawyer's bill is higher than the client expected:

Example One

The statement for professional services that you will find enclosed herewith is, in all likelihood, somewhat in excess of your expectations. In the circumstances, I believe it is incumbent upon me to avail myself of this opportunity to provide you with an explanation of the causes therefor. It is my considered judgment that three factors are responsible for this development.

Example Two

The bill I am sending you with this letter is probably higher than you expected, and I would like to explain the three reasons why.

Example One is awful, is it not? It contains many of the faults we have already discussed—a flock of nominalizations, for example. But notice also the choice of words in Example One. Why does its author say *statement for professional services* instead of *bill*? The client calls it a bill. So does the lawyer, usually. By tradition, the bill itself can be captioned *statement for professional services*. But this is supposed to be a friendly, candid letter to a client; let us call a bill a *bill*.

Why does the author of Example One use *herewith* and *therefor*? To give the letter the scent of old law books? Why does the author use airy, abstract words like *circumstances*, *factors*, and *development*? Do they somehow add dignity? Finally, why does the author use ponderous phrases instead of the simple words used in Example Two:

Example One	Example Two
in all likelihood	probably
in excess of your expectations	higher than you expected
explanation of the causes	explain why

Use Concrete Words

To grip and move your reader's mind, use concrete words, not abstractions. For example, here is how Exodus 7:20–21 describes Moses inflicting a plague on Egypt:

He lifted up the rod and smote the waters of the river... and all the waters that were in the river were turned to blood. And the fish that were in the river died; and the river stank, and the Egyptians could not drink the water of the river; and there was blood throughout all the land of Egypt.

Now suppose that same event were described in the language of a modern environmental impact report:

> The water was impacted by his rod, whereupon a polluting effect was achieved. The consequent toxification reduced the conditions necessary for the sustenance of the indigenous population of aquatic vertebrates below the level of viability. Olfactory discomfort standards were substantially exceeded, and potability declined. Social, economic, and political disorientation were experienced to an unprecedented degree.

The lure of abstract words is strong for lawyers. Lawyers want to be cautious and to cover every possibility, while leaving room to wiggle out if necessary. The vagueness of abstract words therefore seems attractive. Particularly attractive are words like *basis, situation, consideration, facet, character, factor, degree, aspect* and *circumstances:*

> In our present circumstances, the budgetary aspect is a factor which must be taken into consideration to a greater degree.

Perhaps that means "now we must think more about money," but the meaning is a shadow in the fog of abstract words.

Do not mistake abstraction of that sort for the intentional artful vagueness sometimes required in legal writing. For example, judicial opinions sometimes use an intentionally vague phrase to provide a general compass heading when it is not possible to map the trail in detail. In *Bates v. State Bar of Arizona*,[1] the Supreme Court announced that lawyer advertising is protected under the First Amendment commercial speech doctrine. The Court wanted to tell the states that they could regulate truthful lawyer advertising *some,* but not too much. The Court could not then tell how much would be too much, so it said that states may impose *"reasonable restrictions"* on the time, place and manner of lawyer advertising.[2] The phrase was intentionally vague. It gave general guidance, but it postponed specific guidance until specific facts were presented to the Court in later cases.

Intentional vagueness is likewise used in drafting statutes, contracts, and the like, when the drafter cannot foresee every specific set of facts that may arise. But vagueness is a virtue only if it is both necessary and intentional. Knowing when to be vague and when to press for more concrete terms is part of the art of lawyering.

Use Familiar Words

Aristotle put the case for familiar words this way: "Style to be good must be clear.... Speech which fails to convey a plain meaning will fail to do just what speech has to do.... Clearness is secured by using the words...that are current and ordinary."[3] Given a choice between a familiar word and one that will send your reader groping for the dictionary, use the familiar word. The reader's attention is a precious commodity, and you cannot afford to waste it by creating distractions.

Unlike many writers, attorneys usually know who their readers will be, and their choice of words can be tailored accordingly. A patent lawyer who is writing a brief to be filed in the United States Court of Appeals for the Federal Circuit can use legal terms that might be perplexing if used in a letter to the lawyer's inventor-client. Conversely, in writing to the inventor-client, the patent lawyer can use scientific terms that would be hypertechnical if used in a legal brief. In either case, the convenience of the reader must take precedence over the self-gratification of the writer.

Even among familiar words, prefer the simple to the stuffy. Don't say *termination* if *end* will do as well. Don't use *expedite* for hurry, or *elucidate* for explain, or *utilize* for use. Do not conclude that your vocabulary should shrink to preschool size. If an unfamiliar word is fresh and fits your need better than any other, use it—but don't *utilize* it.

Do Not Use Lawyerisms

Lawyerisms are words like *aforementioned, whereas, res gestae,* and *hereinafter.* They give writing a legal smell, but they carry little or no legal substance. When they are used in writing addressed to nonlawyers, they baffle and annoy. When used in other legal writing, they give a false sense of precision and sometimes obscure a dangerous gap in analysis.

A lawyer's words should not differ without reason from the words used in ordinary English. Sometimes there is a reason. For example, the Latin phrase *res ipsa loquitur* has become a term of art[4] that lawyers use to communicate among themselves, conveniently and with a fair degree of precision, about a tort law doctrine.[5] But too often lawyers use Latin or archaic English phrases needlessly. Sometimes they do it out of habit or haste; the old phrase is the one they learned in law school, and they have never taken time to question its use. Other times they do it believing mistakenly that the old phrase's meaning cannot be expressed in ordinary English, or that the old phrase is somehow more precise than ordinary English.

Consider, for example, the word *said* in its archaic use as an adjective. No lawyer in dinner table conversation says: "The green beans are excellent; please pass said green beans." Yet legal pleadings come out like this:

The object of said conspiracy among said defendants was to fix said retail prices of said products in interstate commerce.

Lawyers who use *said* claim that it is more precise than ordinary words like *the,* or *this,* or *those.* They say it means "the exact same one mentioned above." But the extra precision is either illusory or unnecessary, as the above example shows. If only one conspiracy has been mentioned in the preceding material, we will not mistake *this* conspiracy for some other conspiracy, and *said* is unnecessary. If more than one conspiracy has been previously mentioned, *said* does not tell us which of the several is meant. The extra precision is thus illusory. If *the* were put in place of all the *saids,* the sentence would be no less precise and much less clumsy.

Aforementioned is *said*'s big brother, and it is just as useless. "The fifty-acre plot aforementioned shall be divided...." If only one fifty-acre plot has been mentioned before, then *aforementioned* is unnecessary, and if more than one fifty-acre plot has been mentioned before, then *aforementioned* is imprecise. When precision is important, use a specific reference: "The fifty-acre plot described in paragraph 2(f) shall be divided...."

Res gestae is an example of a Latin lawyerism that can obscure a dangerous gap in analysis. Translated, it means "things done." In the early 1800s, it was used to denote statements that were made as part of the transaction in issue (the "things done") and that were therefore admissible in evidence over hearsay objection. Perhaps because *res gestae* is far removed from ordinary English, lawyers and judges began to treat it as a ragbag. They used it carelessly to cover many different kinds of statements made at or about the time of the transaction in issue.[6] With policy and analysis obscured, *res gestae* became little more than a label to express the conclusion that a particular statement ought to be admitted into evidence over hearsay objection. Wigmore said: "The phrase 'res gestae' has long been not only entirely useless, but even positively harmful.... It is harmful, because by its ambiguity it invites the confusion of one rule with another and thus creates uncertainty as to the limitations of both."[7]

The moral is this: do not be too impressed by the Latin and archaic English words you read in law books. Their antiquity does not make them superior. When your pen is poised to write a lawyerism, stop to see if your meaning can be expressed as well or better in a word or two of ordinary English.

♣ Exercise 15

Rewrite these sentences using familiar, concrete words and omitting surplus words.

1. Said defendant International Business Machines Corporation is hereinafter referred to as "IBM."
2. The prisoner's aptitude for acclimatization to lack of confinement is one factor which must be taken into account in the deliberations of the Parole Board.
3. The purpose of paragraph 9(f) is *in ambiguo*, but it appears to be *pro majori cautela*.
4. The effectuation of reform of penal institutions is dependent to some degree upon the extent of awareness of current events in that sector among members of the general populace.
5. The patent laws which give a seventeen-year monopoly on "making, using, or selling the invention" are *in pari materia* with the antitrust laws and modify them *pro tanto*. That was the *ratio decidendi* of the *General Electric* case.

Answers on page 125. More exercises on page 153.

Avoid Shotgunning

When we lawyers want to be precise and cover every possibility, we too often use the shotgun approach—we take rough aim and loose a blast of words, hoping that at least one of them might hit the target. Consider, for example, this criminal statute:

> Every person who...overdrives, overloads, drives when overloaded, overworks, tortures, torments, deprives of necessary sustenance, drink, or shelter, cruelly beats, mutilates, or cruelly kills any animal, or causes or procures any animal to be so overdriven, overloaded, overworked, tortured, tormented, deprived of necessary sustenance, drink or shelter, or to be cruelly beaten, mutilated, or cruelly killed...is guilty of a crime....[8]

The simplest remedy for shotgunning is to use a dictionary and a thesaurus to find a single word that will adequately express the intended meaning.[9] In the statute above, the single verb *"abuse"* could replace the ten-verb shotgun blast.

Sometimes the simple remedy will not suffice. For instance, the author of the animal abuse statute may have feared that a judge would find the single verb *"abuse"* too vague to give the public fair notice of the kinds of conduct covered by the statute. Where vagueness poses a problem, the best course is to choose a serviceable term and define it for the reader.[10] Then, use the term consistently throughout the document, being cautious not to depart from its defined meaning.[11]

In Rule Drafting, Prefer the Singular Number and the Present Tense

When you draft a statute, regulation, bylaw, or other document that states rules, and you have a choice between the sin-

gular and the plural, use the singular unless you can articulate
a sound reason for using the plural.[12]

Do This

A person must not discharge
a firearm inside city limits.

Not This

Persons must not discharge
firearms inside city limits.

The most common reason for using the plural is to refer to a
group of people rather than to individuals within the group.
For example:

Group—Use Plural

The Admissions Director will identify applicants whose college grades indicate high achievement despite adversity.

Individual within a Group—Use Singular

When the Director identifies an applicant whose college
grades indicate high achievement despite adversity, the Director will flag that applicant's file.

Similarly, in rule drafting, use the present tense unless you
can articulate a sound reason for using the past, future, or
other tense.[13]

Do This

If a voter *spoils* his or
her ballot...

A person who *sells* liquor
within two miles of a
college or university...

If contrary information
becomes available, a supp-
lemental response *is*
required.

Not This

If a voter *shall spoil*
his or her ballot...

A person who *has sold* liquor
within two miles of a college
or university...

If contrary information *has*
become available, a supple-
mental response *will be*
required.

One reason for using a tense other than the present tense is to set up a time relationship in the rule. For example, use the appropriate tense for an event that preceded the rule, or an event that will necessarily happen before or after the event you are describing in the rule:

> A member of the armed forces who *was stationed* in a combat zone during the Viet Nam War, but who *did not receive* combat pay, is eligible...

> If a jurisdiction *has adopted* a graffiti abatement program as defined in subsection (f), the court may order the defendant to clean up...

> No interest in property is valid unless it *will vest*, if at all, within 21 years after a life in being at the creation of the interest...

Use Words of Authority with Care

When you draft rules, contracts, and other formal legal documents, be precise and consistent in using words of authority such as *must, shall, will, may, should* and their negative forms, such as *must not*, and *will not*.[14] The biggest troublemaker is *shall*. Sometimes lawyers use it to impose a duty: "The defendant *shall* file an answer within 30 days...." Other times lawyers use it to express a future action ("the lease shall terminate...") or even an entitlement ("the landlord shall have the right to inspect...") Drafting experts have identified several additional shades of meaning *shall* can carry.[15] To make matters worse, many lawyers do not realize how slippery *shall* is, so they use it freely, unaware of the booby traps they are laying for their readers.

The legislative drafters in some jurisdictions in the United States try to tame *shall* by using it only in its command sense: *shall* imposes a duty to do something.[16] In recent years, however, many U.S. drafting authorities have come around to the British Commonwealth view: don't use *shall* for any purpose— it is simply too unreliable.[17]

Throwing out *shall* leaves us with a fairly well-behaved roster of words to express duty, permission, discretion, entitlement, and the like. These words should be used consistently with the meanings stated below:[18]

must	= is required to
must not	= is required not to; is disallowed
may	= has discretion to; is permitted to
may not	= is not permitted to; is disallowed from
is entitled to	= has a right to
should	= ought to
will	= [one of the following:]

        a. (to express a future contingency)

        b. (in an adhesion contract, to express the strong party's obligations)

        c. (in a delicate contract between equals, to express both parties' obligations)

❧ Exercise 16

When you rewrite these passages, pay special attention to your choice of words.

1. All advance payments of rentals made hereunder shall be binding on any direct or indirect assignee, grantee, devisee, administrator, executor, heir, or successor to the lessor.

2. Tenant has not at any time heretofore made, done, committed, executed, permitted or suffered any act, deed, matter or thing whatsoever, whereby or wherewith, or by reason or means whereof the said lands

and premises hereby assigned and surrendered, or any part or parcel thereof are, or is, or may, can or shall be in anywise impeached, charged, affected or incumbered.

3. It shall be and hereby is declared to be unlawful for any person or persons to expel, discharge, or expectorate any mucus, spittle, saliva or other such substance from the mouth of said person or persons in or on or onto any public sidewalk, street, highway, boulevard, thoroughfare, building, terminal, theater, railway train, street car, bus, trolley, ferryboat, steamer, boat, taxicab, jitney or conveyance, or in or on or onto any other public place of whatsoever kind or description, and any person or persons who do so expel, discharge, or expectorate any such substance as defined above at any place herein delineated shall be guilty of a misdemeanor.

4. At any sporting event which involves the participation of an umpire, referee, judge, director, or supervisor in connection with the conduct of such event, it shall be a misdemeanor for any person to offer anything of value to such umpire, referee, judge, director, or supervisor with the intent of influencing the umpiring, refereeing, judging, or supervising of such sporting event in such manner as may affect the outcome thereof.

Answers on page 126. More exercises on page 156.

Notes

1. 433 U.S. 350 (1977).
2. Id. at 384.

3. Aristotle, Rhetoric 1404b, in 11 The Works of Aristotle (W. Ross ed. 1946).

4. "Term of art" is defined on page 21, above. Translated, *res ipsa loquitur* means "the thing speaks for itself." Professor Mellinkoff notes that in tort law, almost everyone understands the phrase to mean at least: "Ordinarily, this sort of thing doesn't happen unless somebody was negligent." David Mellinkoff, Dictionary of American Legal Usage 560–61 (1992).

5. See Restatement (Second) of Torts §328D, comments a) and b) (1965).

6. See, e.g., cases described in Showalter v. Western Pac. R.R., 16 Cal. 2d 460, 106 P.2d 895 (1940).

7. 6 John Wigmore, Evidence §1767 at 255 (Chadbourne rev. ed. 1976).

8. Cal. Penal Code §597(b) (Deering 1997 Supp.).

9. Rudolf Flesch, How to Write Plain English: A Book for Lawyers and Consumers 40–43 (1979).

10. By using a definition, you avoid the need to repeat the shotgun blast time and again. The definition can be either closed-ended or open-ended; each has its advantages and disadvantages. See generally Reed Dickerson, The Fundamentals of Legal Drafting 137–52 (2d ed. 1986).

In the animal abuse example, a closed-ended definition would state: "abuse means..." followed by a list of all the kinds of conduct the statute is intended to cover. One advantage of a closed-ended definition is that it eliminates vagueness. One disadvantage is that the statute will not catch a villain who abuses animals in a manner not listed in the definition. The villain's lawyer will trot out the old Latin phrase *inclusio unius est exclusio alterius* and will argue that the inclusion of some types of abuse was intended to exclude other types of abuse not mentioned.

An open-ended definition would state: "abuse includes but is not limited to..." followed by a list of examples of the kinds of conduct that the statute is intended to cover. One disadvantage of an open-ended definition is that it does not fully cure the vagueness problem. See David Mellinkoff, Legal Writing: Sense & Nonsense 25–26 (1982). One advantage, however, is that the statute will probably catch the villain whose conduct offends the spirit, though not the letter, of the law.

11. Mellinkoff, supra note 10, at 24–26, 136–38.

12. See, e.g., Texas Legislative Council Drafting Manual 100 (1996); Hawaii Legislative Drafting Manual 21 (9th ed. 1996); Louisiana Senate Drafting Manual 39 (1996).

13. G.C. Thornton, Legislative Drafting 103–05 (4th ed. 1996); Texas Legislative Council Drafting Manual 100 (1996).

14. See Bryan A. Garner, A Dictionary of Modern Legal Usage 939–42 (2d ed. 1995); see also Bryan A. Garner, Guidelines for Drafting and Editing Court Rules, 169 F.R.D. 176, 212 (1997); G. C. Thornton, Legislative Drafting 103–05 (4th ed. 1996); Veda Charrow, Myra Erhardt, and Robert Charrow, Clear and Effective Legal Writing 169 (2d ed. 1995).

15. See Joseph Kimble, The Many Misuses of "Shall," 3 Scribes J. Legal Writing 61 (1992); see also Bryan A. Garner, A Dictionary of Modern Legal Usage 940–41 (2d ed. 1995).

16. See, e.g., Arizona Legislative Bill Drafting Manual 84 (1997); Bill Drafting Manual for the Kentucky General Assembly §303 (1996); Louisiana Senate Drafting Manual 38–39 (1996); Texas Legislative Council Drafting Manual 97 (1996).

17. The British Commonwealth view is expressed in Law Commission, Legislation Manual—Structure and Style 43 (1996) (New Zealand); G.C. Thornton, Legislative Drafting 103–04 (4th ed. 1996) (New Zealand); Robert Eagleson & Michele Asprey, Must we Continue with "Shall"? 63 Austl. L. J. 75 (1989) and their sequel, id. at 726 (1989) (Australia); Martin Cutts, The Plain English Guide 36–37 (1995) (Great Britain). U.S. authors who agree include David Mellinkoff, Mellinkoff's Dictionary of American Legal Usage

402–03 (1992) ("unless context can be made crystal clear, prefer *must* or *required* to *shall*"); Bryan A. Garner, A Dictionary of Modern Legal Usage 939–42 (2d ed. 1995); Veda R. Charrow, Myra K. Erhardt, and Robert P. Charrow, Clear and Effective Legal Writing 169 (2d ed. 1995); and Joseph Kimble, The Many Misuses of "Shall," 3 Scribes J. Legal Writing 61 (1992).

18. The chart is a slightly changed version of one contained in Bryan A. Garner, A Dictionary of Modern Legal Usage 942 (1995); see also Bryan A. Garner, Guidelines for Drafting and Editing Court Rules, 169 F.R.D. 176, 212 (1997).

Chapter 8 ————————————————

Avoid Language Quirks

Language quirks are small distractions that draw your reader's mind from *what* you are saying to *how* you are saying it. Most of what lawyers write is read by people, not because they want to, but because they have to. Their attention is therefore prone to wander. Further, they are usually surrounded by outside distractions—the ring of the telephone, the cough at the library table, and the clock that tells them time is short. Language quirks add to those distractions and thus should be avoided.

To take a simple example, most people have been told by some well-meaning teacher never to split an infinitive. An infinitive is split when a modifier is inserted between the word *to* and the verb, for example, "to never split." Even though this "rule" has been thoroughly debunked by experts,[1] it remains implanted in some readers' minds. Those readers will be distracted when they see an infinitive split unnecessarily. Therefore, do not split an infinitive unless doing so will avoid an ambiguity or a clumsy expression.[2] Likewise, do not end a sentence with a preposition unless you have to.

Avoid Elegant Variation

Elegant variation is practiced by writers whose English teachers told them not to use the same word twice in close proximity. Elegant variation produces sentences like this:

> The first case was settled for $20,000, and the second piece of litigation was disposed of out of court for $30,000, while the price of the amicable accord reached in the third suit was $50,000.

The readers are left to ponder the difference between a *case, a piece of litigation,* and a *suit.* By the time they conclude that there is no difference, they have no patience left for *settled, disposed of out of court,* and *amicable accord,* much less for what the writer was trying to tell them in the first place.

Elegant variation is particularly vexing in technical legal writing. The reader of a legal document is entitled to assume that a shift in terms is intended to signal a shift in meaning, and the reader is justifiably puzzled at passages like this:

> The use fee shall be 1% of Franchisee's gross revenue. Franchise payment shall be made on or before the 15th day of each month.

Are *franchise payments* something different from the *use fee?* If so, what are they, and when must the use fee be paid?

Do not be afraid to repeat a word if it is the right word and if repeating it will avoid confusion.

A different, but related, language quirk is the use of a word in one sense and its repetition shortly after in a different sense:

> The majority opinion gives no consideration to appellant's argument that no consideration was given for the promise.

The remedy is obvious—replace one of the pair with a different term:

The majority opinion ignores appellant's argument that no consideration was given for the promise.

Avoid Noun Chains

A long chain of nouns used as adjectives is likely to strangle the reader. That is, noun chains create *noun chain reader strangulation problems.* Bureaucrats love noun chains. They write about *draft laboratory animal rights protection regulations* and about *public service research dissemination program proposals.* Indeed, my own law school once appointed an *Informal Discrimination Complaint Resolution Advisor.*

To bring a noun chain under control, lop off any of the descriptive words that are not essential. If that is not enough, then insert some words to break up the chain, like this: *"draft regulations to protect the rights of laboratory animals."*

Avoid Multiple Negatives

Beware of sentences that contain more than one negative expression. "It shall be unlawful to fail to..." is an example of a double negative. The grammar is proper, but the construction is distracting—it makes the reader's mind flip from *yes* to *no* to *yes.*

In addition to ordinary negative words and prefixes (such as *not, un-,* and *non-*), many other words operate negatively (for example, *terminate, void, denial, except, unless,* and *other than*). If you string a few of these negative words together, you can make the reader's eyes cross, like this:

Provided *however,* that this license shall *not* become *void unless* licensee's *failure* to provide such notice is *unreasonable* in the circumstances.

When you find that you have written a sentence with multiple negatives, identify each negative term. Then pair as many of them as you can to turn them into positives. Finally, rewrite the sentence using as many positives and as few negatives as you can.[3] For instance, "it shall be unlawful to fail to stop at a red light" becomes "you must stop at a red light."

Here is a more complicated passage:

No rate agreement shall qualify under Section 2(a) unless not fewer than thirty days notice is given to all customers; and unless said rate agreement has been published, as provided above, provided however, that the publication requirement shall not apply to emergency rates; and until said rate agreement has been approved by the Commission.

When rewritten in the positive, the passage emerges like this:

To qualify under Section 2(a), a rate agreement must meet these three conditions:

- All customers must receive at least thirty days notice of it; and

- It must be published, as provided above (but emergency rates do not have to be published); and

- It must be approved by the Commission.

Avoid Cosmic Detachment

Every legal problem involves people. Without people, there would be no legal problems. Yet legal writing too often ignores people and addresses itself to some bloodless, timeless cosmic void. For example, here is the opening substantive sentence of the federal copyright law:

Copyright protection subsists, in accordance with this title, in original works of authorship fixed in any tangible medium of expression, now known or later developed, from which they can be perceived, reproduced, or otherwise communicated, either directly or with the aid of a machine or device.[4]

Can you find any people in that sentence? *Authorship* is as close as you can get, and it is none too human.

When you find yourself struggling to express a complex legal idea, remember to ask yourself the key question that you learned in chapter 2: "Who is doing what to whom?"[5] Bring those living creatures into your writing; make them move around and do things to each other. Suddenly abstraction will evaporate, and your writing will come alive.

Remember, too, that your reader is the most important person in the universe—or at least your reader thinks so. Don't be afraid to bring the readers into your sentences, and don't be afraid to call them "you." The personal form of address will help them understand how the passage relates to them.[6]

Use Strong Nouns and Verbs

Most legal writing is declaratory. It simply states the facts, without comment, and without trying to persuade anyone of anything. Statutes, apartment leases, corporate bylaws, and bills of lading fall in this category. But some legal writing does comment. Through commentary, it seeks to persuade the reader to believe what the writer believes. Legal briefs and judicial opinions are obvious examples. Where commentary is appropriate, it will be more potent if you use strong nouns and verbs, not weak nouns and verbs held afloat by adjectives and adverbs. For instance:

Adjectives and Adverbs	Nouns and Verbs
The witness intentionally testified untruthfully about the cargo.	The witness lied about the cargo.
Defendant's sales agents maliciously took advantage of people with little money and limited intelligence.	Defendant's sales agents preyed on the poor and the ignorant.

When you need to use a strong word for commentary, choose one that fits. Do not use a fiery one and then douse it with water:

> rather catastrophic
> somewhat terrified
> a bit malevolently
> slightly hysterical

Similarly, do not choose a flaccid one and then try to prop it up with words like *very* and *quite*:

Weak	Strong
she was very, very angry	she was enraged
this is quite puzzling	this is baffling

Avoid Sexist Language

The very first section of the United States Code says that "words importing the masculine gender include the feminine as well."[7] That may be so in the statute books, but many readers, both women and men, will be distracted and perhaps offended

if you use masculine terms to refer to people who are not necessarily male.[8] On the other hand, many readers will be distracted by clumsy efforts to avoid masculine terms. In recent
years, some legal writers have started using only feminine
terms, but that too is distracting.[9]

Given the nature of the English language, avoiding sex bias
gracefully is no easy task. Here are four suggestions that may
help:

First, don't use expressions that imply value judgments
based on sex. (For example, *a manly effort,* or *a member of the
gentle sex.*)

Second, use sex-neutral terms if you can do so without artifi-
ciality. (For example, use *workers* instead of *workmen* and *reasonable person* instead of *reasonable man.* But don't concoct
artificial terms like *waitpersons* to refer to servers in a restau-
rant.)

Third, use parallel construction when you are referring to
both sexes. (For example, *husbands and wives,* not *men and
their wives,* or *President and Mrs. Kennedy,* not *President
Kennedy and Jackie.*)

Fourth, don't use a sex-based pronoun when the referent
may not be of that sex. For instance, don't use *he* every time
you refer to judges. You can resort to the clumsy phrase *he or
she* in moderation, but you can often avoid the need by using
one of the following devices:

- Omit the pronoun. For example, instead of *"the average
  citizen enjoys his time on the jury,"* you can say *"the average citizen enjoys jury duty."*
- Use the second person instead of the third person. For
  example, instead of *"each juror must think for herself,"*
  you can say *"as a juror, you must think for yourself."*
- Use the plural instead of the singular. For example, instead of *"each juror believes that he has done something*

worthwhile," you can say *"all jurors believe that they have done something worthwhile."*

- Repeat the noun instead of using a pronoun. For example, instead of *"a juror's vote should reflect her own opinion,"* you can say *"a juror's vote should reflect that juror's own opinion."*

- Alternate between masculine and feminine pronouns. For example, if you use *she* to refer to judges in one paragraph, use *he* to refer to lawyers in the next paragraph. Be aware that this device may look artificial; further, if you are careless, you may perform a sex change on somebody in the middle of a paragraph.

- Use the passive voice. For the reasons explained in chapter 4, use this device only in desperation.

❧ Exercise 17

1. When you rewrite this passage, address it directly to the reader and eliminate the elegant variation:

   The Privacy Act of 1974 requires that all governmental units inform each individual whom it asks to supply information: (1) the authority which authorizes the solicitation of the data and whether disclosure of the material is mandatory or voluntary; (2) the principal purpose or purposes for which the information is intended to be used by the agency; (3) the routine uses which may be made of the material; and (4) the effects, if any, of not providing all or part of the data requested by the unit or agency.

2. Break up these noun chains:
   (a) Law office management efficiency seminar

(b) Attorney client trust fund bank account regulations

(c) Cost analysis based proof burden presumptions

3. Eliminate the multiple negatives in this passage:

Except in cases governed by Rule 9.3, no practitioner admitted to the highest court of a sister state shall be denied admission to the bar of this court *pro hac vice*, provided, however, that admission shall be granted only upon motion duly made by a member admitted to practice in this jurisdiction.

4. The following passage is written for the occupants of a high-rise office building, to tell them what to do in an emergency. When you rewrite it, avoid cosmic detachment:

In the event of any fire, explosion, bomb threat, storm, aircraft accident, civil disorder, or other emergency requiring evacuation from the building, whether during normal working hours or thereafter, this building is equipped with klaxon-type warning devices which will be activated. Upon hearing the warning, evacuation is to be by way of the nearest stairwell, proceeding either upward or downward, as directed by the Floor Captain.

5. Put vigor in the following passages by using appropriate nouns and verbs in place of the adjectives and adverbs:

(a) Exposure to asbestos dust can result in very serious illness and can ultimately prove fatal.

(b) Defendant's exceedingly negligent conduct certainly appears to have been the result of an attitude on his part that the safety of his fellow workers was not a matter of very great concern to him.

6. Rewrite the following passages to eliminate the sexist language:
    (a) Even the most honest witness will embellish his story unless you are in control of him at every moment of his questioning.
    (b) Every trial lawyer must develop his own ways to deal with the witness who gives nonresponsive answers to his questions.
    (c) Each witness must be cautioned before giving her testimony that she is to listen to the question carefully and that she is to answer only the questions that have been asked.

Answers on page 126. More exercises on page 157.

Notes

1. See Theodore Bernstein, Miss Thistlebottom's Hobgoblins 116–18 (1971); Henry W. Fowler, A Dictionary of Modern English Usage 579–82 (2d ed. Ernest Gowers 1965).

2. Henry W. Fowler, The New Fowler's Modern English Usage 736–38 (3d ed. R.W. Burchfield 1996); United Press International, Style Book 289–90 (3d ed. 1992).

3. See Rudolf Flesch, How To Write Plain English: A Book for Lawyers and Consumers 94–101 (1979); see also David Mellinkoff, Legal Writing: Sense & Nonsense 28–38 (1982); Robert Eagleson, Writing in Plain English 50–51 (1990).

4. 17 U.S.C. §102 (1994).

5. See page 17, supra.

6. See Eagleson, supra note 3, at 49.

7. 1 U.S.C. §1 (1994).

8. See generally, Ronald Collins, Language, History, and the Legal Process: A Profile of the "Reasonable Man," 8 Rut.-Cam. L.J. 311 (1977); Casey Miller & Kate Swift, Words and Women (1977).

9. See Texas Law Review, Manual on Style 62–63 (8th ed. 1995), which recommends against using either male or female pronouns generically.

Chapter 9 —————————————

Punctuate Carefully

How Punctuation Developed

As English speakers at the threshold of the 21st century, we are accustomed to the idea that punctuation affects meaning, but our punctuation system would have seemed odd to an English speaker in the early 17th century.[1] The punctuation used in those days had evolved from earlier systems of dots, lines, and slash marks used by the Greeks and Romans.[2] The Greek and Roman systems were not syntactic; that is, punctuation marks were not intended to affect meaning and were not based on grammar, as our marks are today. Rather, the Greek and Roman marks served a rhetorical function (by dividing segments of discourse according to formal rhetorical patterns) and an elocutionary function (by indicating where to pause and breathe when reading the text aloud). Like the Greek and Roman systems, the punctuation used in early 17th century English was not syntactic; its function was primarily rhythmic and elocutionary.[3]

By the end of the 17th century, English was starting to become rule-bound. Rules of grammar, spelling, and capitalization developed.[4] About that time, our present syntactic system of punctuation was born. Our syntactic system uses punctuation marks as guides to the grammatical construction and, thus, to the meaning of a passage. Syntactic punctuation does not ignore rhythm and elocution. Shifts in syntax tend to coincide with pauses for emphasis or for breath in oral delivery, and modern punctuation therefore tends to reflect the patterns and rhythms of speech.

Lawyers' Distrust of Punctuation

English-speaking lawyers have traditionally distrusted punctuation as a guide to meaning. Even today in Great Britain, some solicitors prefer to draft legal instruments with almost no punctuation; they argue that punctuation is unreliable because it can capriciously disappear (as when a legal secretary has a momentary lapse of concentration) or capriciously appear (as when a fly explores the page and deposits something that could pass for a comma).[5]

Lawyers' distrust of punctuation as a guide to meaning has three sources. The first was the unreliability of punctuation in the late 17th century, and well into the 18th century, when the syntactic system was in its adolescence. Syntactic punctuation did not spring forth full-grown, nor did every writer adopt it overnight.[6] During this formative period, some writers punctuated for rhythmic and elocutionary effect, some punctuated syntactically, and some did a little of both. Thus, at that time, punctuation was indeed an unreliable guide to meaning.

The second source of distrust was the printing press, which was introduced in England in 1476. Before the printing press, statutes and other important documents were handwritten by professional scribes, and scribes trained by different masters had diverse customs for capitalization, spelling, and punctuation.[7] By the middle of the 17th century, printing had become commonplace, and the printers had a penchant for uniformity. They were known to delete or supply punctuation to make their product uniform.[8] Because the printer may have fiddled with the punctuation, it was an unreliable guide to the author's intended meaning.[9]

The third source of distrust was the old tale that English statutes were traditionally unpunctuated. Professor Mellinkoff long ago exposed that tale as a falsehood. He examined the best available sources of old handwritten statutes and concluded that "English statutes have been punctuated from the earliest days."[10] The punctuation is not like ours; it is often sparse and inconsistent, but it is there. Nonetheless, the old tale lives on and is occasionally still cited in support of a supposed rule that judges can ignore punctuation when they interpret statutes.

Judicial decisions on both sides of the Atlantic yield a rich assortment of conflicting slogans about using punctuation as a guide to meaning. Some say that it should be ignored; others say that it can be used, but only in a pinch. Still others say that it should be considered along with all other available clues to the author's intended meaning.[11] For example, in *United States v. Ron Pair Enterprises*,[12] the United States Supreme Court split 5–4 over the significance of a comma in a bankruptcy statute. One lower federal court had called it a "capricious" comma,[13] and another had called it an awfully "small hook on which to hang a [substantial] change in the law."[14] The majority of five Supreme Court Justices, with no apology, relied partly on the comma to conclude that the statute was clear on its face. The four dissenting Justices, on the other hand, tried to obliterate the comma with a blast of slogans from old cases: punctuation is minor and not controlling, punctuation is not decisive, punctuation is the most fallible standard by which to interpret a writing, and punctuation can be changed or ignored to effectuate congressional intent.

Punctuate Carefully

The lesson that emerges is this: modern readers, including judges, do use punctuation as a guide to meaning. Trying to draft without punctuation is no good because, "if you don't punctuate, a reader will do it for you, in places you never wanted it."[15] Further, leaving the task of punctuation to a legal secretary, as some lawyers are inclined to do, is an abdication of the professional duty to express meaning as clearly as possible.

Thus, when you write, you should punctuate carefully, in accordance with ordinary English usage. The following punctuation guide conforms to ordinary English usage, as expressed in standard modern sources. These sources do not always agree with each other, and where they disagree, I have suggested the approach that will produce clarity with as little complexity as possible. This punctuation guide will not answer *all* of your punctuation questions. For that, your law office library should include at least one reliable, modern text that covers grammar, style, and punctuation.[16]

Definition of Terms

Punctuation is easier if you remember a few definitions:

Subject: The word or group of words that a clause or sentence makes a statement about.

- The *lawyer* had objected to the evidence.

Predicate: The word or group of words that makes a statement about the subject. The complete predicate is the main verb plus any modifiers and complements attached to it.

- The lawyer *had objected to the evidence.*

The simple predicate is the main verb (with its helping verbs).

- The lawyer *had objected* to the evidence.

Phrase: A group of closely related words that does not contain both a subject and a predicate.

- *The lawyer in the gray skirt...*
- *Objecting to the evidence...*

Independent clause: A group of words that contains both a subject and a predicate and that grammatically could stand alone as a complete sentence.

- *The lawyer in the gray skirt objected to the evidence.*

Dependent clause: A group of words that contains both a subject and a predicate, but that grammatically could not stand alone as a complete sentence.

- *When the lawyer in the gray skirt objected to the evidence...*

A dependent clause frequently begins with a subordinating word, such as *who, which, when, that, since,* or *because.*

A dependent clause can function as an adjective, an adverb, or a noun.

- The lawyer *who wore the gray skirt* objected to the evidence. [adjective—describes lawyer]
- *When she objected,* the judge sustained the objection. [adverb—tells when]
- The judge agreed *that the evidence was inadmissible.* [noun—tells what]

Commas

We begin with commas, because commas (or the lack of them) cause more mischief in the law than all of the other punctuation marks combined.

Use a comma when you join independent clauses with a coordinating conjunction

An independent clause can stand on its own as a complete sentence. When you use a coordinating conjunction (*and, but, or, for, nor, yet,* and *so*) to join two independent clauses into one sentence, put a comma before the conjunction.

- The defendant intentionally accessed the government computer system, and he intentionally denied access to authorized users.

- The "worm" that the defendant inserted in the computer system multiplied a million-fold, yet the defendant claimed that he did not intend to damage the system.

To join two independent clauses properly, you need both the comma and the conjunction. (If you use only the comma without the conjunction, you will be guilty of a "comma splice," a grievous sin.) Another way to join two independent clauses properly is with a semicolon; when you do that, you ordinarily do not use a conjunction.

- The defendant's computer sabotage cost the government at least ten thousand hours of lost computer time; it also destroyed valuable, irreplaceable data.

Use a comma after introductory elements

Put a comma after an introductory phrase or clause.

- Wanting to settle the case quickly, the plaintiff authorized her lawyer to accept any amount over $5,000.

- At the time of the accident, the defendant was intoxicated.

- To make the point clearly, she used a diagram.

If the introductory element is very short, omit the comma.

- At home he wears glasses instead of contact lenses.

Omit the comma if the introductory element is followed by inverted word order.

- From the apartment above came a loud scream.

Use commas to set off nonrestrictive elements

A nonrestrictive element within a sentence modifies or describes part of the sentence but is not essential to the meaning of the sentence. Set off nonrestrictive elements with commas. Elements beginning with *which, although,* or *though* are usually nonrestrictive.

- The car, which is blue, ran the red light.

In contrast, a restrictive element is essential to the meaning of the sentence, and it should not be set off with commas. Elements beginning with *that, because, before, while, if,* or *when* are usually restrictive.

- The car that ran the red light was blue.

To determine whether an element is restrictive or nonrestrictive, try mentally eliminating it from the sentence. If the meaning changes, or the sentence becomes ambiguous, the information is restrictive and should *not* be set off with commas.

- His father, who is an engineer, arrived on Tuesday.
- The corporation, which has its principle place of business in Alaska, is engaged in oil and gas exploration.
- The job that she was seeking was filled.

When a dependent clause comes at the beginning of a sentence, always put a comma at the end of it, even if it is restrictive.

- If you accept our conditions, we will postpone the hearing.

Use commas to set off parenthetical elements

When you insert a parenthetical element into a sentence, put a comma on both ends of it. A parenthetical element is one that is pertinent but not essential to the meaning of the sentence. If a word, phrase, or clause could be deleted without affecting the meaning of the sentence, then set it off with commas.

- The mayor's indictment was, to say the least, unexpected.
- Freedom of speech is, after all, one of our most cherished rights.

Legal citations included in the text are parentheticals and should be set off by commas.

- In the *DeShaney* case, 489 U.S. at 192, that very point was discussed by the Court.

Use commas to separate the items in a series

When a sentence contains a series of three or more items joined with one conjunction, put commas after each item except the last.

- The defendant was armed with a sawed-off shotgun, a semi-automatic pistol, and a hunting knife when he entered the bank.

If the series is simple and commonly used, you can omit the comma before the conjunction.

- The American flag is red, white and blue.

If the series is complicated or contains internal commas, use semicolons rather than commas between the items.

- The police search of the suspect's apartment produced engraving plates, which were of the type used for counterfeiting; a large quantity of ink, which apparently had been stolen from the government's ink supplier; and a variety of forged passports and other travel documents, which showed that the suspect had recently traveled to nine European countries.

Use commas to separate coordinate adjectives

When two or more adjectives are "coordinate," they modify a noun equally, and they should be separated with commas. Do not put a comma between the last adjective and the noun.

- The plaintiff was driving an old, rattly, blue truck.

If the last adjective and the noun together form the term that is modified by the prior adjectives, do not use a comma before the last adjective.

- The plaintiff was driving an old, rattly Ford truck.

If one adjective modifies another, do not separate them with a comma. To tell whether the adjectives are equal modifiers (and thus should be separated with commas), try mentally rearranging the adjectives or mentally inserting the word *and* between the adjectives. If the meaning does not change, the adjectives are equal modifiers (coordinates), and you should use a comma to separate them.

- A dark, cold night (*dark* and *cold* modify *night* equally).
- A bright red tie (*bright* modifies *red*; a "red, bright tie" states a different meaning).
- A strong constitutional argument (*constitutional argument* is the term modified by *strong*).

Use commas to set off transitional or interrupting words and phrases

Use commas to set off transitional words (*therefore, thus, furthermore, moreover,* and the like) at the beginning or in the middle of a sentence.

- The conclusion, therefore, is that attorney advertising deserves only limited protection under the First Amendment.

If the transitional word is between two independent clauses, put a semicolon in front of it and a comma after it.

- Attorney advertising is a type of commercial speech; therefore, it deserves only limited protection under the First Amendment.

If a term of direct address (*madam, sir, my friend,* and the like) interrupts a sentence, set it off with commas.

- We submit, Your Honor, that the injunction should be lifted.

Use commas to set off dates, titles, geographic names, and short quotations

Respected modern sources differ about the use of commas in writing dates. Here are some commonly recommended formats:

- Tuesday, July 6, 2007, is apparently the termination date.
- Apparently 6 July 2007 is the termination date.
- Apparently July 2007 is the termination date.

Titles that follow a person's name are usually nonrestrictive and should be set off with commas.

- Jane Sherwood, M.D., testified for the defense.

- Jake Michaels, Esq., is the youngest partner.

Use commas to separate geographic place names (cities from states, and states from nations).

- Seattle, Washington, is the defendant's principal place of business.
- Tokyo, Japan, is the defendant's principal place of business.

Use a comma to introduce a short quotation, unless it is incorporated into your sentence.

- The witness said, "The red car was speeding."
- The statute banned smoking "in any public building."

Semicolons

Some writers put semicolons and wild mushrooms in the same category: some are nice, and some are not, and since it is hard to tell the difference, they should all be avoided. Semicolons are not, in fact, hard to master, and they can be very useful.

Use a semicolon to join two independent clauses without a conjunction

You can use a semicolon without a conjunction to join two closely related independent clauses; doing so adds variety to your writing and helps keep it from seeming choppy. Do not, however, join two independent clauses with a semicolon unless they are closely related.

- The defense counsel objected to the question; she said that it called for information protected by the attorney-client privilege.

- Plaintiff Munoz had just witnessed his wife's death; he was in a state of deep shock.

Use a semicolon when two independent clauses are joined by a transitional expression

When you use a transitional expression (such as *therefore, however, furthermore, thus, indeed, in fact, as a result,* or *for example*) to join two independent clauses, put a semicolon before the transitional word or phrase, and put a comma after it.

- The court granted the preliminary injunction; therefore, the company could not fire the plaintiff while the case was pending.

- The witness had no personal knowledge of the event; in truth, her testimony was hearsay.

- Her testimony could have been admitted under several exceptions to the hearsay rule; for example, either the excited utterance exception or the contemporaneous statements exception would apply.

Use semicolons to separate the items in a complicated series

Ordinarily you should use commas to separate the items in a series, as explained above. But, if the series is complicated or contains internal commas, use semicolons to separate the items.

- The prosecutor called the following witnesses: Susan Wu, a psychiatrist; Michael Bradford, a ballistics expert; and George Frye, a police investigator.

Colons

A colon indicates that what follows is a summary or elaboration of what precedes it, or is a series, or is a long quotation.

Use a colon to introduce a series

When you use a colon to introduce a series, the material that precedes the colon must be able to stand alone as an independent clause.

The independent clause can include *as follows* or *the following*, but it need not do so.

- We must subpoena the following witnesses: Barnes, Cruz, and Younger.

- We must subpoena three witnesses: Barnes, Cruz, and Younger.

Do not put a colon between a verb and its object or between a preposition and its object.

- We must subpoena: Barnes, Cruz, and Younger. (The colon is misused here because it separates the verb *subpoena* from its three objects.)

- We must serve a subpoena on: Barnes, Cruz, and Younger. (The colon is misused here because it separates the preposition *on* from its three objects.)

Use a colon to introduce a summary, elaboration, or illustration

- The plaintiff failed to prove two key elements: negligence and proximate cause.

- The damages were staggering: $1,948,000 in medical bills and $74,000 in lost wages.

- Only one thing stands between us and settlement: money.

You can also use a colon to join two independent clauses if the first clause introduces the second, or if the two clauses have a cause and effect relationship.

- The DNA evidence is vital: it is our only proof that the defendant was at the scene.

- The gasoline truck hit the wall: the gasoline explosion killed the driver.

Use a colon to introduce a long quotation

You should ordinarily use a comma to introduce a short quotation, but if the quotation is longer than one sentence, then use a colon.

- She invoked the words of Abraham Lincoln: "The Lord prefers common-looking people. That is the reason He makes so many of them."

Dashes

Use dashes to signal an abrupt break

Commas, parentheses, and dashes are all used to set off material that interrupts a sentence. The three differ in the emphasis they give to the material they set off. Commas tend to be neutral; they neither emphasize nor play down the material. Parentheses tend to play down the material, to make it clearly subordinate. Dashes tend to emphasize the material.

- The judge—bristling with indignation—slammed his gavel on the bench.

- We need not reach the constitutional issue—that can await another day and another set of facts.

Use dashes, not commas, when you need to clearly set off a lump of material that needs to sit in the middle of a sentence because of what it modifies.[17]

- The magistrate may rule on any procedural motion—including a motion to suppress evidence and a motion to allow or disallow discovery—at any time following the acceptance of a plea.

Parentheses

Use parentheses to set off interjected or explanatory material

Like commas and dashes, parentheses can be used to set off material that interrupts a sentence. Parentheses tend to play down the material that is set off, to make it clearly subordinate.

- The police found a diamond ring (worth at least $1,000) in the suspect's pants pocket.

The material inside the parentheses should be punctuated as necessary.

- In the suspect's pants pocket, the police found a diamond ring (worth at least $1,000) and three credit cards (a Mastercard, a Visa card, and an American Express card).

Use parentheses to avoid ambiguities

Used in moderation, parentheses (and their big brothers, brackets) can be helpful when you need to clarify what modifies what, or to interject a brief definition or qualification, or to state an exception.

- [The levy established in subparagraph 9 does not, however, apply to residential property (property used by a taxpayer as a primary residence).]
- No deduction is allowed if the donor retains or transfers an interest (as defined above) in the property to any person other than the donee spouse (or the estate of the spouse).

Use parentheses when you want to label the items in a series

When a sentence lists several complex elements in a series, you can use numbers or letters enclosed in parentheses to indicate the intended divisions.

- The testator gave her sister-in-law three items: (a) 100 shares of AT&T common stock, (b) the amethyst ring that had belonged to the testator's Aunt Dolores, and (c) an ancient calico cat, which had been the testator's constant companion.

Use parentheses to introduce shorthand expressions you will use later

- The Eastern Region Trade Agreement (ERTA) prohibits any retaliatory tariff on agricultural commodities.
- Universal Communications, Inc. (UCI) developed the transverse uniflex modulator system ("the system") in 1994.

Apostrophes

Use apostrophes to form possessives

Modern authorities differ on how to form some possessives.

Be aware that reasonable people can disagree passionately about the following rules (one wonders whether there are not grander things to worry about). To make the possessive of a singular noun, add 's, even if the word ends with an s sound. If that would make a triple s sound, then use an apostrophe only. For classical and biblical names that end in s, use an apostrophe only.

- Susan's opera cape
- Theodore James's new novel
- Defendant Jones's fingerprints
- Achilles' heel
- Zacharias' son, John the Baptist

To make the possessive of a plural noun that ends in an s sound, use an apostrophe only. If the plural ends in a different sound, use 's.

- The women's restroom
- The Joneses' house
- The clans' movement across the desert

If more than one owner is listed, you must decide whether the ownership is joint or individual. For joint ownership, form the possessive for the last owner listed. For individual ownership, form the possessive for each owner listed.

- Jesse's and Ula Mae's computers (each owns one)
- Bruce and Tim's sailboat (they own it together)

For compound expressions, form the possessive with the last element listed.

- The plaintiff was driving her mother-in-law's car.
- Your Honors' original order required payment of costs. (several judges entered the order)

Never put an apostrophe in a possessive pronoun (his, hers, its, yours, ours, theirs, whose). Remember that *its* is the possessive pronoun meaning "belonging to it." *It's* is the contraction for "it is." Finally, if your ear tells you that a possessive sounds awkward, be bold and use a few glue words to form the possessive the long way. For example, "the index of the revised and expanded edition" is longer but sounds better than "the revised and expanded edition's index."

Use 's to form the plural of some terms

Use *'s* to form the plural of abbreviations, numbers, letters, symbols, and words referred to as words. The modern trend is not to use an apostrophe in the plurals of years.

- Revise this contract by replacing all the aforementioned's with this's.
- The witness recalled that the license number included three 6's.
- She got mostly B's in law school.
- C.P.A.'s usually enjoy the tax courses.
- The Impressionists dominated the late 1800s.

Use apostrophes in contractions and abbreviations

In contractions and abbreviations, an apostrophe stands for the omitted letters. For example, *can't, it's, wouldn't, Nat'l,* and *Ass'n.* Because contractions convey informality, you should not use them in drafting statutes, court orders, contracts, appellate briefs, or other formal legal documents. They are, however, appropriate if you want a piece of legal writing to have an informal tone. For example, some judges favor contractions in jury instructions because the informal tone is consistent with their personal style in delivering the instructions orally to the jury. They are also appropriate if you want to set an informal tone in a client letter, an office memorandum, or even in a chatty law review article.

Hyphens

Check compound terms in an up-to-date dictionary

Some compound terms (terms that are formed from more than one word) are written as separate words (*ice cream*), some are hyphenated (*brother-in-law*), and some are written as a single word (*textbook*). Usage often changes over time. A compound term usually enters the language as two words (*hard disk*). As it becomes more familiar, it often grows a hyphen (*freeze-dried*). When it becomes commonplace, it often becomes one word (*handlebar*). When you are in doubt, check the term in an up-to-date dictionary.

Follow common usage in hyphenating compound modifiers

If two or more words act together as a single modifier, they should usually be joined by hyphens. Some of these compound modifiers are common and can be found in a dictionary (*second-guess*), but others are created to fit the need (*nursing-home care*). The following general principles, plus a large measure of your own common sense, will help avoid hyphen errors like this one: "The new tax deduction is designed to aid small business owners." (Apparently the large ones must fend for themselves.)

Hyphenate only when the modifier precedes the term modified.

- My hard-headed boss

- My boss is hard headed.

Do not hyphenate if the first term is an adverb ending in *-ly*.
- An overly active imagination
- A radically different constitutional analysis

Do not hyphenate foreign phrases.
- A bona fide purchaser
- An ex post facto law

A hyphen is usually used with the prefixes *ex-*, *self-*, *quasi-*, and *all-*. A hyphen is usually not used after the prefixes *anti, co, de, inter, intra, multi, non, para, pro, re, semi,* or *super*— unless the second element is capitalized or the hyphen is needed to avoid confusion.
- Her ex-husband
- A self-inflicted wound
- The quasi-contract claim
- Antitrust law
- The anti-Communist forces
- Her paralegal assistant
- His redrafted brief

If two or more hyphenated compounds share a common element, the shared element can be used only once.
- Long- and short-term budget reductions
- Pre- and post-judgment interest

Use hyphens for compound numbers and fractions

Use hyphens for numbers twenty-one through ninety-nine, even if they are part of a larger number.

- Thirty-eight
- One hundred thirty-eight

Use hyphens between all elements of a fraction.

- A one-third contingent fee
- A one-twenty-sixth share

Use a hyphen to divide a word at the end of a line

When you must break a word at the end of a line, use a hyphen, and make the break between syllables. Check your dictionary for the syllable divisions. Word processing programs that insert hyphens automatically are not infallible, so stay alert. Do not divide a word over a page break or leave a one-letter syllable standing lonely on the end of a line. By the way, you can avoid the whole issue by using a ragged (unjustified) right-hand margin, which also makes reading easier for some people and which avoids distracting oddities in the spacing between words.

Periods, Question Marks, and Exclamation Points

Use a period to end a declarative sentence, a command, or an indirect quotation

- Serve the interrogatories today.
- She asked what day the interrogatory answers are due.

Follow common usage in putting periods in abbreviations

Some abbreviations use periods, and others do not. You can find most common abbreviations in a good dictionary, and the tables at the back of the Bluebook[18] contain the ones commonly used in legal writing. If you cannot find it in either of those sources, you probably should not use it because your reader may not know what you are talking about. If an abbreviation with a period at the end comes at the close of a sentence, use only one period.

Use a question mark to end direct questions

Put a question mark at the end of a direct question.

- Is hate speech protected by the First Amendment?
- What would justify a writ of mandamus in this case?

Do not put a question mark at the end of a request or command that is courteously phrased as a question.

- Will you please have the memorandum to me by tomorrow.
- Would counsel kindly take his feet off the table.

Do not put a question mark at the end of an indirect question.

- The judge asked why our brief exceeded the page limit.
- Why, she said, did we file such a long brief.

Use exclamation points rarely

Exclamation points, which show surprise or strong emotion, are much like chili peppers. Used sparingly and in the right context, they add a piquant touch, but be careful. In formal legal writing, such as an appellate brief, exclamation points are almost never appropriate because they tend to be strident rather than persuasive. But, in a client letter or office memorandum, the occasional exclamation point will do no harm; if nothing else, it lets the writer blow off steam.

Quotations

Enclose short, direct quotations in quotation marks

Use double (") quotation marks to surround direct quotations of under fifty words. Alternate between double and single (') marks for material quoted within a quotation. For quotations of fifty words or more, indent on both the left and right, and leave any internal quote marks the way you found them in the original. Put commas and periods inside quotation marks; other punctuation marks belong outside unless they are part of the quoted material.

Indicate deletions, alterations, and additions to quoted material

Use square brackets around anything you add to or change in a quotation, such as when you add an explanatory word, or change a plural to a singular, or change a letter from upper to lower case, or vise versa. An ellipsis (...) is three periods separated by spaces and with a space at each end. Generally, use an ellipsis to indicate an omission. Do not, however, use an ellipsis to begin a quotation, and do not use ellipses when you are quoting only a phrase or clause, rather than a full sentence.[19]

❧ Exercise 18

1. Correct the punctuation and wording to make the following into properly constructed sentences.

    (a) Future investments, designed to upgrade the production of chemicals with higher product values and to expand selectively into new chemical markets.

(b) Working capital consisting of cash and marketable securities, accounts and notes receivable, inventories, and other current assets, net of current liabilities.

(c) Historically, funds from operations having served as the company's principal source of capital, but supplementing this source have been additions to long-term debt.

2. Correct the punctuation errors in these sentences.

(a) Information retrieval presents even more difficult problems in major cases and there is no way of corporate counsel knowing in advance just what will be required and when.

(b) Two comments are appropriate, first, experts in document retrieval quite probably are already in the employ of the corporation itself.

(c) Second, why should the attorneys in large, modern corporations use antiquated methods of retrieval, their business colleagues having the most advanced equipment and techniques available?

(d) Litigators of the old school may oppose the use of modern retrieval methods they argue that an adversary's task in discovery will be that much easier.

(e) This may be a consequence, of course, it is even possible that an adversary may gain access to the system itself and thus find out what questions to ask.

(f) But this is a small price to pay for the benefits

granted, the greatest danger to the corporate client is not knowing the facts.

3. Correct the comma errors in these sentences.

   (a) The objective is to define when the responsibility for care custody and control of the plant is transferred from the Contractor to the Company.

   (b) The plant or a part thereof, is ready for commissioning after erection and successful testing, and when the Company agrees that all contract requirements have been fulfilled.

   (c) After the Company agrees that the plant is ready for commissioning the Company will perform all maintenance operating adjustments, and settings, that may be required except that all repairs and changes, required to meet the contract terms, will be performed by the Contractor.

   (d) The Company will notify the Contractor within ninety, (90), days, of any failure to meet the performance guarantees.

4. Add commas or other punctuation to these sentences where necessary.

   (a) Exploratory costs including geophysical costs delay lease rentals and exploratory dry hole costs are expensed as incurred.

   (b) Costs of acquiring nonproducing acreage are capitalized and costs of such acreage that become productive are amortized by field on a unit-of-production basis.

   (c) The corporation shall indemnify to the full extent authorized or permitted by the laws of the State of Delaware any person made or threatened to be made a party to an action or proceeding (whether civil criminal administrative or investigative) by reason of the fact that he his testator or intestate is or was a director officer or employee of the corporation or served any other corporate function.

5. Revise the punctuation in these sentences.

   (a) Bill Siapno, a trim, 54-year-old geologist, is the head of marine sciences for Deepsea Ventures, a firm whose goal is to retrieve three million tons, a year, of mysterious, blackish, mineral lumps, called "manganese nodules" from the abyssal plains of the Pacific Ocean.

   (b) These sooty, crumbling, irregularly shaped, lumps contain more than 40 elements.

   (c) The growing specter of mineral shortages and cartels, as well as the promise of corporate profits, spurred Deepsea Ventures, a consortium of oil, mining, and metal manufacturing companies, to tackle the difficult task of lifting nodules through three vertical miles of cold, dark, water.

6. Some of these sentences have semicolon errors. Correct them.

   (a) After the plaintiff class had been certified; the judge entered an order requiring all discovery to be completed by March 30th.

   (b) Plaintiffs filed their final set of interrogatories on March 25th; the judge ruled that they were too late.

   (c) The ruling was entirely justified; in fact, the judge might well have imposed monetary sanctions on plaintiffs' counsel.

(d) Sanctions are proper when counsel have intentionally violated a discovery order; when counsel have negligently failed to comply with time deadlines; and when counsel have delayed discovery, without good faith, by other means.

7. Some of these sentences have colon errors. Correct them.

   (a) This court therefore decrees that the following items belong to plaintiff Black Sands: the field known as River Cloud, including well A-2; the profits from all production in the River Cloud field, including well A-2, from March 13, 1998, to the date of this decree; and a one-half interest in the field known as New Hope.

   (b) The Bill of Rights is more than a list of aspirations: it is a contract between the people and their government.

   (c) The doctrine of *res judicata* includes: merger, bar, and collateral estoppel.

   (d) Some of the common law privileges are: the attorney-client privilege, the communications privilege between spouses, and the privilege of the clergy.

8. Some of these sentences have errors in the use of dashes, commas, and parentheses. Correct them.

   (a) Punching the pretrial order with his forefinger the trial judge said, "No a thousand times no you may not call Dr. Ferdley as an expert witness on the damage issue!"

   (b) The following financial statements include the operations of Magnatec International, Ltd., a limited partnership between Magnatec, Inc., and

Austerflatz, S.A., a Swiss enterprise that does business only in Turkey.

(c) Price fixing a violation of the Sherman Act as well as price discrimination which is prohibited except in some limited situations by the Robinson Patman Act and tying agreements which can be illegal under either the Sherman or Clayton Acts are all explained in the company's new handbook for sales representatives.

(d) He asserted that only one thing caused the downfall of communism economic inefficiency.

9. Some of these sentences have apostrophe and spelling errors. Correct them.

(a) Tomorrows assignment is on the blackboard.

(b) In contracts and torts, both teacher's assignments are sometimes unclear.

(c) Two witnesses testimony is necessary in treason cases.

(d) A witness' testimony must be based on personal knowledge.

(e) Judge's traditionally wear black robes because it adds to the proceedings dignity.

(f) The winning argument was her's not his'.

(g) Sams and Virginia's papers are on the table.

(h) Of all the papers, their's were outstanding.

(i) Its necessary to cover every possible contingency.

(j) Professor Simmons's tax article is on reserve.

(k) Some state's statutes' don't even mention the problem.

(l) Whose going to clarify it if the legislature's dont?

(m) A business gross profits can be taxed under the old law.

(n) Profit's are sometimes a poor measure of success.

(o) The police asked who's gun it was.

(p) Joe Samuels dog bit the postmen's leg.

(q) When it's teeth sank in, the postmans howls could be heard all the way up to the Jameses house.

(r) Degas's career flourished in the 1890s.

Answers on page 127. More exercises on page 160.

Notes

1. Parts of this chapter are drawn from Richard Wydick, Should Lawyers Punctuate?, 1 Scribes Journal of Legal Writing 7 (1990). The history of punctuation in legal writing is related in David Mellinkoff, The Language of the Law 152–70 (1963).

2. See Joseph Robertson, An Essay on Punctuation 1–14 (1785), reproduced in facsimile, English Linguistics 1500–1800, No. 168 (1969); Robert Peters, A Linguistic History of English 298–99 (1968).

3. See Simon Daines, Orthoepia Anglicana 70–73 (1640), reproduced in facsimile, English Linguistics 1500–1800, No. 31 (1967); see also George Puttenham, The Arte of English Poesie 74 (Willcock & Walker ed. 1936), explained in Mindele Treip, Milton's Punctuation and Changing English Usage 1582–1676, 27–28 (1970).

4. See Albert Baugh & Thomas Cable, A History of the English Language 253–94 (3ed. 1978); Barbara Strang, A History of English 104–55 (1970).

5. See Wydick, supra note 1, at 7–10. Reed Dickerson, a respected U.S. authority on legal drafting, similarly distrusted punctuation. He said the careful legal drafter should use punctuation as a "finishing device," but "should not rely solely on it to do what an arrangement of words can do." Reed Dickerson, The Fundamentals of Legal Drafting 188 (2d ed. 1986).

6. See Treip, supra note 3, at 16–17, 35–53.

7. See Strang, supra note 4, at 107–10, 157–59.

8. See, e.g., Percy Simpson, Shakespearian Punctuation 7–15 (1911); Treip, supra note 3, at 14–34.

9. See Mellinkoff, supra note 1, at 163.

10. Mellinkoff, supra note 1, at 157–64.

11. See authorities collected in Wydick, supra note 1, at 19–22.

12. 489 U.S. 235 (1989).

13. In re Dan-Ver Enter., 67 Bankr. 951 (W.D. Pa. 1986).

14. In re Newbury Cafe, 841 F.2d 20, 22 (1st Cir. 1988), vacated and remanded sub nom., Massachusetts v. Gray, 489 U.S. 1049 (1989).

15. David Mellinkoff, Legal Writing: Sense & Nonsense 57 (1982).

16. The choices are legion and include the following: The Chicago Manual of Style (14th ed. 1993); United Press International Stylebook (3d ed. 1992); Frederick Crews, The Random House Handbook (6th ed. 1992); Andrea Lunsford and Robert Connors, The St. Martin's Handbook (2d ed. 1992); and James Howell and Dean Memering, Brief Handbook for Writers (3d ed. 1993).

17. Bryan A. Garner, Guidelines for Drafting and Editing Court Rules, 169 F.R.D. 176, 195 (1997).

18. The Bluebook: A Uniform System of Citation (16th ed.

1996), compiled by the editors of the Columbia Law Review, the Harvard Law Review, the University of Pennsylvania Law Review, and the Yale Law Review.

19. For more detailed guidance on quotations in legal writing, see id.

Appendix One

Reader's Exercise Key

These are not *the* answers to the exercises. They are some of the many possible answers. You may often find that your answers are better than the ones given here. That should be cause for cheer, not puzzlement.

♣ Exercise 1

Caution: The distinction between working words and glue words is rough-hewn, and reasonable people can disagree about particular words in a sentence. Therefore, do not be puzzled if your answers differ in places from those suggested here.

1. Here is the original sentence with the working words underlined:

   The <u>testimony</u> that was <u>given</u> by <u>Reeves went</u> to the <u>heart</u> of the <u>defense</u> that <u>he asserted</u>, which was <u>his lack</u> of the <u>specific intent</u> to <u>escape</u>.

   The original sentence could be revised to read:

   Reeves's testimony went to the heart of his defense, that he had no specific intent to escape.

117

With the working words underlined, the revised sentence looks like this:

> Reeves's testimony <u>went</u> to the <u>heart</u> of <u>his defense</u>, that <u>he had no specific intent</u> to <u>escape</u>.

2. Here is the original sentence with the working words underlined:

> In the <u>event</u> that there <u>is</u> a <u>waiver</u> of the <u>attorney-client privilege</u> by the <u>client</u>, the <u>letters must be produced</u> by the <u>attorney</u> for the <u>purpose</u> of <u>inspection</u> by the <u>adversary party</u>.

The original sentence could be revised to read:

> If the client waives the attorney-client privilege, the attorney must produce the letters for inspection by the adversary party.

With the working words underlined, the revised sentence looks like this:

> <u>If</u> the <u>client waives</u> the <u>attorney-client privilege</u>, the <u>attorney must produce</u> the <u>letters</u> for <u>inspection</u> by the <u>adversary party</u>.

❧ Exercise 2

1. The parties were in complete agreement about the amount of rent due and about the due date.

2. For simplicity, an ordinary deed of trust would be the best.

3. Because of the *Burke* decision, the savings clause was added to avoid any ambiguity.

4. In fairness, we should not apply the new rule retroactively.

5. When the funds are received, we will transfer title, hoping to clear up all questions about this matter.

6. I cannot now recall what the letter was about.

❧ Exercise 3

1. When the judgment is entered...

2. Here estoppel can be invoked...

3. He was sentenced to the county jail for five months...

4. By the terms of our contract...

5. No doubt the statute applies where...

6. The claim was clarified by a bill of particulars.

7. The trial judge must consider whether...

8. This offer will stand until you...

9. Usually the claimant's good faith is not disputed...

10. The plaintiff filed the complaint even though she knew that...

11. Arbitration is sometimes useful if the parties...

12. This point has troubled many courts...

13. Because he was injured...

❧ Exercise 4

1. Appellant's opening brief contains three misstatements of fact.

2. The witness need not sign the deposition transcript until the errors are corrected.

3. In approving a class action settlement, the court must guard the interests of absent class members.

4. We cannot tell whether trial counsel's misconduct influenced the jury verdict.

5. We served our first set of interrogatories nine weeks ago.

❧ Exercise 5

We turn now to plaintiff's request for an injunction. The defendant argues that an injunction is unnecessary, because the exclusionary clause is already void under this court's prior order. Since the exclusionary clause can have no further effect, the defendant argues that we can give the plaintiff complete relief without an injunction. Defendant's argument has obvious merit. Thus we have decided not to issue an injunction.

❧ Exercise 6

1. Section 1038 pertains to any contract that provides for attorney fees.

2. Discovery can commence before the judge considers the motion.

3. We agree with your position, but if you intend to cause delay, we will oppose you.

4. To improve downstream water quality, we must stop polluting the headwaters.

5. If this breach continues, my client will terminate the contract immediately.

6. We could amend the interrogatory answer, but if we do so now, the court may suspect our client's good faith.

7. This court cannot fulfill the testator's wishes unless it invalidates the *inter vivos* transfer.

8. We seek to cooperate with you, and we hope that you will change your position. If you refuse to do so, and if you do not complete the work on schedule, we will impound your funds.

❧ Exercise 7

1. The verb "was questioned" is passive.

2. The verb "has petitioned" is active. The verb "will...be denied" is passive.

3. The verb "had been granted" is passive. The verb "would...face" is active.

4. The verb "has existed" is active.

5. The verb "pioneered" is active. The verb "has been rejected" is passive.

6. The verb "suggests" is active. The verb "should... have been admitted" is passive.

❧ Exercise 8

1. An attorney who receives clients' funds must put them in the Client Trust Account.

2. Either party may terminate this agreement by giving thirty days notice to the other party.

3. Each month the defendant manufacturers exchanged price lists, and they agreed to make all sales at list price or above.

4. If my husband does not survive me by thirty days, I give my children whatever items of my personal property my executor selects for them.

5. The supplier insisted that the goods were of merchantable quality.

6. In some cases you must fill out Form 242A before we can clear you through customs. We will not clear you through customs until the Immigration Officer approves your Form 242A. If the Immigration Officer decides that you do not need to fill out Form 242A, then we will clear you through customs promptly.

❧ Exercise 9

1. Class actions serve an important function in our judicial system. They permit claims of many individuals to be resolved at the same time. This avoids repetitious litigation and gives claimants a way to enforce claims that are too small for individual litigation.

2. Consumers are sometimes abused and exploited by false, misleading, or irrelevant advertising. But that does not necessarily require the government to intrude into the marketplace. Consumers themselves can go to court, as can competing sellers who lose business because of such advertising.

3. The majority opinion ignores an important fact: the states are sovereigns, both in common law and in federal constitutional law. Therefore, claims made by states are not generally subject to legal doctrines such

as laches, acquiescence, estoppel, or statutes of limitations of the type in issue here.

❧ Exercise 10

1. A response must be filed with the hearing officer within twenty days after the petition is served.

2. The attorney-client privilege applies to the client's revelation of a past crime. But it does not apply when the client seeks the attorney's aid to plan to carry out a future crime.

3. The sole eyewitness saw the accident from a seventh floor window, half a block north of the intersection. She testified that she did not see which car entered the intersection first.

4. Plaintiff's grandfather, Jose Cruz, later transferred the disputed 200 acres by a deed of gift that was bitterly contested by the heirs but that was ultimately upheld by the probate court.

❧ Exercise 11

Unless the claim is framed as a federal question, venue would be proper in any of these judicial districts:

a. the Southern District of New York, if the plaintiff resides there; or

b. the Eastern District of California, if the defendant does business there; or

c. the Northern District of Illinois, if the events in question took place there.

🐝 Exercise 12

1. Only expensive therapy can alleviate plaintiff's pain.

2. The attorney argued that his client, being ignorant of the law, should receive a light sentence.

3. Defendant's argument overlooks a 1994 amendment to the statute.

4. Only when the claim is brought without good faith can attorney fees be awarded under Section 309.

5. The special tax provision was apparently intended, in the eyes of Congress, to encourage the production of cotton.

🐝 Exercise 13

1. Appellant must have recognized the weakness of its claim. It was represented by Bishop & Donald, counsel of long experience in government contract litigation, a field that requires no small degree of expertise.

2. The proposed legal ethics rule would require an attorney to place all funds received on behalf of a client in the attorney's client trust account. That would include an advance for attorney fees not yet earned, but it would not include a flat fee paid in advance.

🐝 Exercise 14

1) The freshwater vessel tax must be paid on the following vessels over 18 feet in length:
   a) sailboats, and
   b) inboard motor boats.

2) The bar can discipline an attorney who is convicted of a misdemeanor that involves moral turpitude, or is convicted of any felony.

3) The state hearsay rule defines "former testimony" to mean testimony taken under oath at:

   a) an earlier hearing in the same or a different case; or

   b) a deposition taken in the same or a different case; or

   c) any other formal adjudicative proceeding conducted by a governmental agency.

❧ Exercise 15

1. The defendant International Business Machines Corporation is here called "IBM."

A simpler way is to show the abbreviation in parentheses after the proper name is used the first time: "Defendant International Business Machines (IBM) contracted with plaintiff…"

2. One thing the Parole Board must consider is the prisoner's ability to get used to freedom.

3. The purpose of paragraph 9(f) is unclear, but it seems to have been included as an extra precaution.

4. Prison reform depends partly on how much the public knows about what is happening in prisons.

5. The patent laws, which give a seventeen-year monopoly on "making, using, or selling the invention," concern the same general subject as the antitrust laws, and the two should be construed together. The patent laws modify the antitrust laws to some extent. That is why *General Electric* was decided as it was.

❧ Exercise 16

1. All advance payments of rent under this lease are binding on the lessor's successors in interest.

2. Tenant has done nothing that would give anyone a claim against the leased premises. [This exercise and the answer are taken from George Hathaway, An Overview of the Plain English Movement for Lawyers, 62 Mich. Bar J. 945 (1983).]

3. It is a misdemeanor for any person to spit in a public place.

4. It is a misdemeanor for any person to offer anything of value to an umpire, referee, judge, director, or supervisor of a sporting event with the intent to influence the outcome of the sporting event.

❧ Exercise 17

1. The Privacy Act of 1974 says that each federal agency that asks you for information must tell you the following:
   • its legal right to ask for the information and whether the law says that you must give it;
   • what purpose the agency has in asking you for it and the use to which it will be put; and
   • what could happen if you do not give it.

[This exercise and the answer are taken from Fine Print, p. 1 (Jan. 1980), published by the Document Design Center of the American Institutes for Research, Washington, D.C.]

2. (a) Seminar on efficient management of law offices.
   (b) Regulations concerning bank accounts maintained by attorneys for client trust funds.

(c) Presumptions affecting the burden of proof based on cost analysis.

3. Except as provided in Rule 9.3, any practitioner who is admitted in the highest court of a sister state shall be admitted to the bar of this court pro hace vice, upon motion by a member who is admitted to practice in this jurisdiction.

4. In an emergency, you will hear a loud horn. Go to the nearest stairs, and do what the Floor Captain tells you.

5. (a) Exposure to asbestos dust can cause grave injury or death.

(b) Defendant's recklessness was caused by his callous disregard for the safety of his fellow workers.

6. (a) Even the most honest witness will embellish the story unless you are in control at every moment of questioning.

(b) As a trial lawyer, you must develop your own ways to deal with the witness who gives nonresponsive answers to your questions.

(c) All witnesses must be cautioned before giving their testimony that they are to listen carefully to the questions and that they are to answer only the questions that have been asked.

🐾 Exercise 18

The punctuation errors in Exercise 18 could be corrected in a variety of ways; remember that these answers show only *one* of the correct ways to do it.

1. (a) Future investments are designed to upgrade the production of chemicals with higher product val-

ues and to expand selectively into new chemical markets.

(b) Working capital consists of cash and marketable securities, accounts and notes receivable, other current assets (net of current liabilities), and inventories. (The word order was changed to make clear that the phrase in parentheses modifies only "current assets.")

(c) Historically, funds from operations have served as the company's principal source of capital, but additions to long-term debt have supplemented this source.

2. (a) Information retrieval presents even more difficult problems in major cases, and there is no way of corporate counsel knowing in advance just what will be required and when.

(b) Two comments are appropriate. First, experts in document retrieval quite probably are already in the employ of the corporation itself.

(c) Second, why should the attorneys in large, modern corporations use antiquated methods of retrieval when their business colleagues have the most advanced equipment and techniques available?

(d) Litigators of the old school oppose the use of modern retrieval methods; they argue that an adversary's task in discovery will be that much easier.

(e) This may be a consequence, of course. An adversary may even gain access to the system itself, and thus find out what questions to ask.

(f) But this is a small price to pay for the benefits granted; the greatest danger to the corporate client is not knowing the facts.

3. (a) The objective is to define when the responsibility for care, custody, and control of the plant is transferred from the Contractor to the Company.

   (b) The plant, or a part thereof, is ready for commissioning after (1) erection and successful testing, and (2) when the Company agrees that all contract requirements have been fulfilled.

   (c) After the Company agrees that the plant is ready for commissioning, the Company will perform all required maintenance operating adjustments and settings, except that all repairs and changes that are required to meet the contract terms will be performed by the Contractor.

   (d) The Company will notify the Contractor within ninety (90) days of any failure to meet the performance guarantees.

4. (a) Exploratory costs (including geophysical costs, delay lease rentals, and exploratory dry hole costs) are expensed as incurred.

   (b) Costs of acquiring nonproducing acreage are capitalized, and costs of such acreage that become productive are amortized by field on a unit-of-production basis.

   (c) The corporation shall indemnify, to the full extent authorized or permitted by the laws of the State of Delaware, any person who is made (or threatened to be made) a party to an action or proceeding (whether civil, criminal, administrative, or investigative) because he (or his testator or intestate) is (or was) a director, officer, or employee of the corporation or served any other corporate function. (Better still, divide this mess into several short sentences.)

5. (a) Bill Siapno, a trim, 54-year-old geologist, is the head of marine sciences for Deepsea Ventures, a firm whose goal is to retrieve three million tons a year of mysterious, blackish mineral lumps called "manganese nodules" from the abyssal plains of the Pacific Ocean.

   (b) These sooty, crumbling, irregularly shaped lumps contain more than 40 elements.

   (c) The growing specter of mineral shortages and cartels, as well as the promise of corporate profits, spurred Deepsea Ventures (a consortium of oil, mining, and metal manufacturing companies) to tackle the difficult task of lifting nodules through three vertical miles of cold, dark water.

6. (a) After the plaintiff class had been certified, the judge entered an order requiring all discovery to be completed by March 30th.

   (b) Plaintiffs filed their final set of interrogatories on March 25th; the judge ruled that they were too late.

   (c) The ruling was entirely justified; in fact, the judge might well have imposed monetary sanctions on plaintiffs' counsel.

   (d) Sanctions are proper when counsel have intentionally violated a discovery order; when counsel have negligently failed to comply with time deadlines; and when counsel have delayed discovery, without good faith, by other means.

7. (a) This court therefore decrees that the following items belong to plaintiff Black Sands: the field known as River Cloud, including well A-2; the profits from all production in the River Cloud field, including well A-2, from March 13, 1998, to the

date of this decree; and a one-half interest in the field known as New Hope.

(b) The Bill of Rights is more than a list of aspirations: it is a contract between the people and their government.

(c) The doctrine of res judicata includes merger, bar, and collateral estoppel.

(d) Some of the common law privileges are the attorney-client privilege, the communications privilege between spouses, and the privilege of the clergy.

8. (a) Punching the pretrial order with his forefinger, the trial judge said, "No, a thousand times no, you may not call Dr. Ferdley as an expert witness on the damage issue!"

(b) The following financial statements include the operations of Magnatec International, Ltd. (a limited partnership between Magnatec, Inc., and Austerflatz, S.A., a Swiss enterprise that does business only in Turkey).

(c) Price fixing (a violation of the Sherman Act), as well as price discrimination (which is prohibited, except in some limited situations, by the Robinson Patman Act), and tying agreements (which can be illegal under either the Sherman or Clayton Acts) are all explained in the company's new handbook for sales representatives. (Better still, the sentence should be divided into several shorter sentences.)

(d) He asserted that only one thing caused the downfall of communism—economic inefficiency.

9. (a) Tomorrow's assignment is on the blackboard.

(b) In contracts and torts, both teachers' assignments are sometimes unclear.

(c) Two witnesses' testimony is necessary in treason cases.

(d) A witness's testimony must be based on personal knowledge. (There is no triple *s* sound here.)

(e) Judges traditionally wear black robes because they add to the proceedings' dignity. (*Proceedings* is a plural noun.)

(f) The winning argument was hers, not his.

(g) Sam's and Virginia's papers are on the table.

(h) Of all the papers, theirs were outstanding.

(i) It's necessary to cover every possible contingency.

(j) Professor Simmons's tax article is on reserve.

(k) Some states' statutes don't even mention the problem.

(l) Who's going to clarify it if the legislatures don't?

(m) A business's gross profits can be taxed under the old law. (There is no triple *s* sound here.)

(n) Profits are sometimes a poor measure of success.

(o) The police asked whose gun it was.

(p) Joe Samuels's dog bit the postman's leg.

(q) When its teeth sank in, the postman's howls could be heard all the way up to the Jameses' house.

(r) No changes.

Additional exercises follow.

Appendix Two

Additional Exercises

🦫 Exercise 1A

In each sentence below, underline the working words. Then rewrite the sentence, underline the working words, and compare your results with the original.

1. We believe that the conclusion that emerges in the light of this history is that every presumption should be on the side of the preservation of rights granted by the common law.

2. On the assumption that there is an absence of statutory language that would lead us to a contrary conclusion, it is our belief that preservation of rights to which the parties have become entitled under common law is the course of action most consistent with sound social policy.

3. It is the fact that heroin totaling one hundred grams and cocaine totaling fifty grams were discovered by the agents at the time of the arrest of the appellant.

4. This fact, standing alone, however, fails to compel one to reach the conclusion that there existed probable

cause for the agents to believe that use had been made of the van owned by appellant for the transportation across state lines of the said heroin and cocaine.

5. It is frequently the case that a state will not be able to—and is certainly not required to—draw the lines that demark the boundaries of voting districts, and other political units as well, in a manner that creates divisions of people on the basis of characteristics that have a bearing on likely political behavior.

6. There are two situations where courts could sensibly reach a decision that the presence of this fifth component is not necessary in order to make the legislature's category sufficiently narrow to pass muster under the Constitution.

7. The situation is presently, of course, in flux, and in the fullness of time it is entirely possible that these orders providing limited injunctive relief may turn out to have been only the first steps in the development of a broad judicial prohibition of the kind of conduct that is in question in this case.

8. One might voice the objection that *Lochner v. New York* and the other cases cited above that follow *Lochner* protected the "economic rights" of businessmen whereas in contrast, *Roe v. Wade* protects a "human right." It is to be noted, however, that not all of the cases in the *Lochner* series involved regulation of economic matters, and even those that did involve economic regulation resist application of the "big business" stereotype with which they are commonly associated by the commentators. Moreover, it is significant to observe that in some of the cases, the employer's "liberty of contract" claim was joined by the employee, who was aware of the fact that if it were necessary for him to be employed on the terms set by

the law that was at issue in the case, then employment would be entirely out of the question.

❧ Exercise 2A

Rewrite these sentences, omitting surplus words and avoiding compound constructions.

1. With respect to plaintiff's third claim, namely that there was a breach of warranty, the lower court held that by reason of the Uniform Commercial Code, which was applicable with reference to the sale, there could be no recovery.

2. The testimony of an economist, Dr. Bronovski, was offered for the purpose of undercutting plaintiff's evidence with respect to injury by reason of lost sales.

3. In order to prevail on a motion for summary judgment, the defendants must make a clear showing in terms of the lack of disputed issues of fact.

4. In reference to the allegations set forth in Paragraph 13, please identify by means of the date, author's name, and recipient's name, all laboratory reports written subsequent to June 29, 1998, but prior to February 25, 2001, in connection with studies conducted for the purpose of ascertaining the chemical composition of the allegedly infringing compounds.

5. From the point of view of judicial economy, defendant's petition should be denied in accordance with the principle that interlocutory appeals are disfavored. In the event that the defendant ultimately loses at trial, it can appeal at that point in time with a view to challenging the trial judge's ruling, inasmuch as no preju-

dice is suffered prior to the time of entry of a final judgment.

6. In the event of a breach on the part of Lessee of any of the covenants set forth in paragraphs 9 through 10 of this Lease Agreement, all payments specified under the provisions of paragraphs 3(a) and 3(b) shall immediately become due and payable.

7. I am in receipt of your letter of August 13th in reference to my client's copyright infringement claim. With the exception of your assertion as respects the possible applicability of the "fair use" doctrine, my client and I are in agreement with everything you say.

8. On behalf of both myself and my law partners, I am writing for the purpose of expressing our sorrow in reference to the unfortunate death of your husband, who was not only our partner but, in addition to that, our dear friend, and who, rest assured to know, will deeply be missed on the part of all of us here at the firm.

9. As I mentioned during the course of our recent telephone conversation, under the provisions of our partnership agreement with your late husband, the firm will henceforth, commencing on the fifteenth day of this month, and thereafter for the period of three years, be sending you a monthly check in the amount of $8,500, which reflects the death benefit payments to which you are entitled pursuant to the terms of the partnership agreement.

10. In the interest of minimizing your tax liability in connection with these monthly death benefit payments, you should feel no hesitation about contacting our tax partner, Marylou Hunter, who will be glad to assist you without charge with reference to this matter.

❧ Exercise 3A

Revise these sentences to omit the word-wasting idioms and other surplus words.

1. At that point in time, the deputies were not conducting a "search," even though it is the fact that they were looking through the windows of the car.

2. This is an instance in which Federal Rule of Evidence 803 would allow the admission of public records, insofar as they are relevant.

3. It is certainly not the case that every union political activity can escape scrutiny simply because of the fact that the First Amendment protects free speech.

4. It is of equal importance in this instance that the employees should not be able to secure the benefits of the contract for the period of the strike, until such time as they are willing also to accept the burdens thereof.

5. There is no doubt but that the inspector was justified by the obvious nervousness of the skipper in this case in demanding that the cargo be opened for further examination of its contents in an effort to answer the question as to whether there was contraband aboard.

6. In the case of a taxpayer who intentionally fails to report the item as income, this is an instance in which criminal prosecution would be appropriate.

7. If the situation is that the employer has made good faith efforts to comply with the statutory requirements, that should surely be considered, because it is not the case that the Department must prosecute every offender.

8. In the instance at hand, if attorney Lutz was aware of the fact that Ms. Bowles was employed in the Sales Di-

vision of the adversary corporation, then it was a situation in which he should have obtained consent of adversary counsel before interviewing her with respect to matters in connection with the litigation.

9. Except for the fact that the Swiss excise tax applies to imported luxury automobiles, we would be of the opinion that the proposal would be revenue-neutral.

10. If it should happen that the Supreme Court denies certiorari, as is the case in the majority of instances, then jurisdiction with respect to the matter of the sentencing issues will revert to the state trial court.

11. If it had been the case that the termite inspectors had caught the problem at the time when they made their initial inspection, my client would have been alerted to the fact that other timbers in close proximity to the soil line had the possibility of being infested as well.

12. Your recent letter to my law partner, Adella Knight, concerning the matter of the legal fees incurred in connection with our firm's representation of you in your civil action against Untermeyer Corporation has been brought to my attention by Ms. Knight.

13. In her dissent, Justice Hughes made the argument that during the period from 1967, which was the year of enactment by Congress of the original statute, through to the year 1998, when the adoption of the amendment occurred, an excessive number of cases were delegated to an inadequate number of magistrates, the majority of whom lacked the ability to manage a heavy caseload.

14. In view of the fact that in the immediate future it is probable that we will be in a position to respond affirmatively, it would appear at the present point in time that there is no need for us to decide the question as to

whether there may be different circumstances in which a negative response would be the more prudent course.

♠ Exercise 4A

Rewrite these sentences, omitting surplus words and focusing on the actor, the action, and the object of the action.

1. There were four grounds stated in the *Perault* case for ordering the involuntary partition.

2. Since the purchase money has been delivered, it is now the appropriate time for us to close the escrow account.

3. Absent a claim of fraud, there is no way for plaintiff to avoid the plain language of the statute.

4. It is difficult for us to imagine a clearer case of abuse of process.

5. It is obvious that there is no factual basis for the second cause of action, and there is apparently no doubt but that plaintiff's attorneys realized that.

6. There are three types of law that were formerly ignored by the German scholars.

7. It is now recognized, even by the German scholars, that (the same as a statute) a judicial decree is an exercise of the law-making power of the State.

8. It is possible to understand how much statutes are at the mercy of the courts by examining the many meanings judges have discovered in the Statute of Frauds.

9. There are instances in which the judges on the King's Bench make new law just as freely as does Parliament itself.

10. Although there are rules and maxims for the interpretation of statutes, it is obvious that their generality leaves much to the practical wisdom of the courts.

❧ Exercise 5A

In the following passages you will find all the kinds of surplus words discussed in chapter 2. Rewrite them, omitting as many surplus words as you can.

1. [*The following is typical of the language used by old-fashioned lawyers in court pleadings where they want to incorporate some earlier allegations into a later allegation.*] Plaintiff realleges and incorporates herein by reference each and every allegation contained in paragraphs ___ through ___ of the _____ cause of action as if fully set forth herein. [See Irwin Alterman, Plain and Accurate Style in Court Papers 49 (1987).]

2. With respect to the use of evidence in regards to a person's character, there are certain basic principles that are familiar ground for each and every trial lawyer.

   First, in the case of litigation which is concerned with civil claims, evidence relating to a person's character is not admissible when offered for the purpose of proving in what manner the said person acted on a particular occasion. Pursuant to this rule, should driver D cause the death of pedestrian P by driving over P, the plaintiff in a civil action charging D with the wrongful death of P could not introduce evidence about or concerning D's character in regards to driving in a wild manner as proof of how D drove on the occasion in question.

Second, in respect to litigation involving charges of violations of the criminal law, the general rule recited above is likewise applied, excluding situations in which certain statutes and rules have created exceptions with regard to instances in which the general rule is not applied. Thus, supposing it to be the case that in the example described above, driver D were charged with vehicular manslaughter in connection with the death of pedestrian P. By application of the general rule, evidence offered in the prosecution's case-in-chief for the purpose of proving D's character as respects wild driving would not be admissible as circumstantial proof of the manner in which D drove on the occasion in question.

❧ Exercise 6A

Revise the following, eliminating surplus words and using base verbs in place of nominalizations.

1. Settlement of the MacroTec patent litigation is essential, but our commencement of discussions with the MacroTec people must not carry the appearance of desperation as respects our situation.

2. It could possibly be the case that an honest expression to MacroTec of our desire to undertake exploration of possible areas of future research cooperation with them could be the perfect inducement to serious deliberation about amicable termination of the patent cases.

3. Maintenance of the corporation's liquidity is dependent, not only on the forbearance of its major creditors, but also on renewal of our efforts to achieve a near-term expansion of sales in the approximate range of 10%.

4. Lodestar Express acted in contravention of its collective bargaining agreement with Trucking Employees Local 108 when it simultaneously effected the closure of the Dorrington warehouse and the transference of jobs to the Lorrimer facility.

5. Lodestar's termination of full-time drivers at Dorrington, coupled at the same point in time with the creation of new part-time, low compensation positions at Lorrimer, was a violation of its union contract and also a main cause of the perpetuation of Lodestar's reputation as a corporation prone to banditry.

6. Plaintiff bases its next argument on its contention that this case should be governed by a rule of per se illegality. With respect to some categories of restraints on trade, the courts have reached the conclusion that application of a per se rule is appropriate. In the situations to which a per se rule is applied, it is the intention of the courts to foreclose the defendant from any contention that the restraint of trade is reasonable in the circumstances. The per se rule has a tendency to operate unfairly in those instances where justification of the restraint may be found in economic efficiencies the achievement of which would be an impossibility in the absence of the restraint. We have reached the conclusion that justice would be ill served by application of a per se rule to the case at hand.

❧ Exercise 7A

Underline the verbs in the following sentences. (Note that some of the sentences have more than one verb.) Then identify each verb as either active voice or passive voice.

1. If a writing has been used by a witness to refresh her memory before testifying, the adverse party is entitled to see the writing and to use it in cross-examining the witness.

2. If a writing accurately records what a witness perceived, and if the writing was prepared while the witness's memory was fresh, and if the witness no longer remembers what she perceived, then the hearsay exception for past recollection recorded may apply.

3. If the past recollection recorded exception has been held applicable by the trial judge, the writing may then be read aloud to the jury, but it will not be shown to the jury nor taken into the jury room during deliberations.

4. In the Fitch case, the defendant was convicted of the rape of victim A, and part of the evidence that had been used against him was a prior conviction for the rape of victim B.

5. Defendant Fitch appealed, arguing that the due process clause is violated when one sex offense is used as evidence of an evil disposition to commit another sex offense.

6. Fitch's argument was based on 150 years of precedent, but that precedent has been jettisoned by the legislature's decision to change the evidence law in sexual assault cases.

✿ Exercise 8A

Rewrite these sentences, omitting surplus words, using base verbs instead of nominalizations, and using the active voice. Supply any missing information that you need.

1. If undue risk is to be avoided in your law practice, it must be remembered that attorney malpractice suits are becoming increasingly common, and ample malpractice insurance is regarded as a necessity by most prudent lawyers.

2. The jurors should be respected by attorneys, but undue solicitude should be avoided. An attorney's posture of fawning deference or attempts to curry favor are resented by jurors.

3. Within three days after a Preliminary Notice of Default has been filed by Owner, cancellation of all outstanding credit vouchers shall be made by Lender or Lender's agents.

4. Good faith efforts to purge the contempt by respondent shall be taken into consideration by the court when the sentence is set.

5. If no request for legal services has been made, and if the proposal of legal representation is made initially by the lawyer, the solicitation rule may have been violated.

6. The line which is drawn by ABA Model Rule 7.3 is not the same as the First Amendment line that was drawn in the lawyer solicitation cases decided by the United States Supreme Court.

7. Initiation of personal contact with a potential client by a lawyer is prohibited by ABA Model Rule 7.3 in those instances in which a significant motivation for the initiation of personal contact is the lawyer's hope of personal financial gain.

8. The argument made by Learned Hand was that, at the time of the emergence of the Constitution from the Convention in 1787, one's examination of its text would offer no basis for drawing the inference that the Execu-

tive and the Legislature were to be bound by interpretations of the Constitution made by the Supreme Court.

9. However, Judge Hand argued, it could plainly be seen that the collapse of the whole scheme would be a near certainty unless the final word as respects matters of constitutionality could be spoken by one of the three branches with binding effect upon the other two.

10. The Constitution was rescued, according to the view expressed by Judge Hand, by application of an ancient maxim of statutory construction, to wit: that interpolation of a provision into a text is always permissible to prevent the defeat of the legislative venture at hand.

11. Thus, the conclusion reached by Hand was that interpolation into the Constitution of the power of judicial review was not a lawless act by the Supreme Court.

12. One lesson that has been taught to me by years of past experience is that disagreement with Learned Hand is the sheerest folly.

13. Nonetheless, the argument made here is that the text of the Constitution itself can be looked to as authorization for the power of judicial review, and that mere interpolation is not necessary.

14. The commencement of my argument is in the text of the Supremacy Clause, wherein it is stated that the Constitution (together with federal statutes made in pursuance of the Constitution and treaties made under U.S. authority) shall be the supreme law of the land and that "the judges in every State shall be bound thereby." *

---

* Items 8–14 are a mutilated version of sentences in a famous article by Professor Herbert Wechsler. After you revise them, you can see how he wrote them originally in Toward Neutral Principles of Constitutional Law, 73 Harv. L. Rev. 1 (1959).

❧ Exercise 9A

Rewrite these passages using short sentences and omitting as many surplus words as you can.

1. In this law library there is hereafter to be no smoking, except in the lounge on the third floor which has been specifically set aside for that purpose, and there is to be no consumption of either food or drink in any portion of the law library, however eating and drinking are permitted in the snack bar area located in the basement.

2. Seeking to support the judgment on additional grounds not passed on by the Court of Appeals, but which have been argued here both orally and in the briefs, as was proper by reason of the fact that these grounds raise only issues of law and do not call for examination or appraisal of evidence, respondents assert that the contracts were in violation of the Wages and Hours Act.

3. Upon consideration of the motion made by plaintiff in the above entitled action to compel the defendant herein to answer certain questions posed to her at a deposition properly noticed and taken in the within action, and upon consideration of the defendant's opposition thereto, and having heard the arguments of counsel in open court, and having considered the entire record on file herein, and having concluded that the deposition questions in issue are relevant to the within action, or are likely to lead to the discovery of admissible evidence, and are not objectionable on the ground that they call for information that would be protected by any privilege granted by statute or the common law, it is, therefore

ORDERED AND DECREED that plaintiff's motion be, and hereby is, granted; and it is further

ORDERED AND DECREED that defendant shall appear and answer the deposition questions which are the subject of the said motion at a date to be set by mutual agreement of counsel for the plaintiff and counsel for the defendant herein; and it is further

ORDERED AND DECREED that defendant shall pay to plaintiff the sum of $1,000, said amount reflecting costs and a reasonable attorney fee incurred by plaintiff in pursuing the above motion as aforesaid.

4. [The following is Rule 11(g) of the Federal Rules of Appellate Procedure, as of 1997.] *Record for Preliminary Hearing in the Court of Appeals.* If prior to the time the record is transmitted a party desires to make in the court of appeals a motion for dismissal, for release, for a stay pending appeal or on a supersedeas bond, or for any intermediate order, the clerk of the district court at the request of any party shall transmit to the court of appeals such parts of the original record as any party shall designate.

5. No person shall loiter in any public place with the intent to commit prostitution, as evidenced by acting in a manner and under circumstances which openly demonstrates the purpose of inducing, enticing, or soliciting prostitution, or procuring another to commit prostitution, including but not limited to repeatedly beckoning to, stopping, or engaging in conversations with passersby, or repeatedly stopping or attempting to stop motor vehicles by hailing the drivers, waiving arms, or making any other bodily gestures, or circling an area in a motor vehicle and repeatedly beckoning to, or contacting pedestrians or motorists in a sexually

suggestive manner. Violation of this provision constitutes a Class Two misdemeanor.

6. The doctrine known as "law of the case" provides that
where, upon appeal, the Supreme Court in deciding
the appeal, states in its opinion a principle or rule of
law necessary to the decision, that principle or rule of
law becomes the law of the case and must be adhered
to throughout its subsequent progress, both in lower
court and upon subsequent appeal, as well as in any
subsequent suit for the same cause of action, even if in
its subsequent consideration the Supreme Court may
clearly be of the opinion that the former decision is er-
roneous, subject however to the qualifications that the
point of law involved must have been necessary to the
prior decision, that the matter must have been actually
presented and determined by the Supreme Court in the
prior decision, and that the application of the doctrine
will not result in an unjust decision.

❧ Exercise 10A

Close the gaps in each sentence by moving the intervening
words or by splitting the sentence in two. When you rewrite,
omit surplus words and rearrange the thoughts into logical
order.

1. Plaintiff's complaint, containing nine causes of action
including slander, invasion of privacy, intentional interference with prospective business advantage, and
intentional infliction of emotional distress, was filed
last Tuesday.

2. Intentional interference with prospective business advantage, although related to a more familiar tort known

generally by the name interference with contract, or intentional interference with contractual relations, or inducement of breach of contract, does not require proof that the defendant interfered with a presently existing contract.

3. Plaintiff's intentional interference claim alleges, in language typical of the lawyers in the firm of Hungerdunger, Hungerdunger, & Hungerdunger who are serving as plaintiff's counsel and who are known throughout this jurisdiction for the purpleness, as well as the opacity of their prose, business losses of one million dollars.

4. Our best line of defense against the intentional interference claim, which is not defective on its face but which has absolutely no basis in fact, is promptly to take the deposition of the plaintiff and then to make, using the admissions that we will undoubtedly be able to extract from the plaintiff, a motion for partial summary judgment.

5. I pass by with brief mention another expedient, Cessio in Jure by name, having the same object as the last, which, though it did not immediately make its appearance in English history, was of immemorial antiquity in Roman law.

6. It is clear that without an inquiry into the reasons which underlie (or may underlie) the enforcement of promises generally, these questions cannot be answered.

7. Possession by the defendant, without a reasonable explanation consistent with innocence, of property that has been determined by the jury from all the facts and circumstances to be recently stolen permits an inference to be drawn by the jury that the defendant knew the property was stolen.

8. A remainder, regardless of when it becomes posses-
sory, complies with the Rule against Perpetuities as
soon as it vests. Thus B's interest, in a devise to A for
life, remainder to A's children for their lives, remainder to B, is presently vested, though clearly it may
not come into possession (well beyond the period of
perpetuities) until the death of a child of A yet un-
born.

☙ Exercise 11A

Use tabulation to clarify these passages. When you rewrite,
omit surplus words.

1. If you have accrued 5 years of service in the home office, or 3 years of service in a field office, excluding,
however, a field office located within 20 miles of your
permanent residence; or, if you have served not less
than 2 out of the most recent 4 years in an overseas office (except the overseas offices in Paris, Madrid, and
Bonn) and were not accompanied by your dependents,
you are eligible for the Paid Leave of Absence Program; excepting, however, executive officers (Pay
Scale EX6 or above), clerical employees (Pay Scale CB
or below), and persons not qualified for Section A
benefits.

2. Except as otherwise provided in these rules, every
order required by its terms to be served, every plead-
ing subsequent to the original complaint unless the
court otherwise orders because of numerous defendants, every paper relating to discovery required to be
served upon a party unless the court otherwise orders,
every written motion other than one which may be

heard ex parte, and every written notice, appearance, demand, offer of judgment, designation of record on appeal, and similar paper shall be served upon each of the parties. [This exercise is not a joke; see Fed. R. Civ. P. 5(a).]

❧ Exercise 12A

Rewrite these sentences to solve the modifier problems. If a sentence has more than one possible meaning, select whichever one you wish and rewrite the sentence to express that meaning unambiguously.

1. Being constantly alert for signs of mechanical or dynamic injury, the deceased is examined by the pathologist to determine the cause of death.

2. A skilled pathologist is able to distinguish between structural changes produced by trauma and those produced by disease through years of training and experience.

3. In gunshot cases, a determination must be made whether the wound was inflicted before or after death by the pathologist.

4. Because of lack of mass and velocity, the pathologist will usually have difficulty with projectiles fired by small caliber pistols.

5. A pathologist can express an educated guess only on the probable cause of death.

❧ Exercise 13A

Rewrite these sentences without the nested modifiers. As you rewrite, omit surplus words.

1. Medical insurance, which in the case of union members is covered by a five-year contract hammered out a few months ago through collective bargaining, is among the company's most generous fringe benefits.

2. Computation of the amount to be entered on line 23 can be accomplished by subtracting the amount entered on line 14, which is obtained by adding the amounts on lines 5, 6 (but not more than $1,000), and 7, from the amount entered on line 22.

3. Any respondent who is required to submit to the Agency, pursuant to Regulation 9(c) in the case of an individual, or pursuant to Regulation 9(d) in the case of a corporation, partnership or other business entity, any information which is claimed by the respondent to include trade secrets or other material that must be kept in confidence by the Agency, in accordance with Regulation 10(b), must notify the Agency in writing of that claim at the time of the submission.

4. Any person who believes a particular hazardous substance intended or packaged in a form suitable for use in the household or by children should be exempted from full label compliance otherwise applicable under the act, because of the size of the package or because of the minor hazard presented by the substance, may submit to the Commission a request for exemption under section 3(c) of the act, presenting facts in support of the view that full compliance is impracticable or is not necessary for the protection of the public health.

Exercise 14A

Clarify the reach of the modifiers in these sentences. If a sentence has more than one possible meaning, select whichever one you wish and revise the sentence to express that meaning unambiguously.

1. For purposes of the psychotherapist-patient privilege, the term "psychotherapist" means not only M.D. psychiatrists and psychologists licensed under the Medicine and Health Code, but also state certified clinical social workers, family counselors, and school psychologists.

2. A lawyer may withdraw from representing a client if the client persists in a course of action that the lawyer considers repugnant or imprudent, or persists in a criminal or fraudulent course of action that involves the lawyer's services, or persists in failing to discharge an obligation to the lawyer, if the lawyer has given the client reasonable warning that the lawyer will withdraw if the client does not relent.

3. Employee promises not to misappropriate, copy, or disclose any trade secret, manufacturing instruction, laboratory manual, quality control manual, or customer list that has been identified by Employer as *Confidential* or *Restricted*.

❧ Exercise 15A

Rewrite these passages using familiar, concrete words and omitting surplus words.

1. Judgment upon any arbitration award that may be rendered herein may be entered in any court having jurisdiction thereof.

2. The within Agreement constitutes the entire understanding and agreement between the Parties hereto with respect to the subject matter hereof, and no modification or amendment hereof shall be valid or binding upon the Parties hereto unless said modification or amendment is made in writing and signed on behalf of each of the said Parties by their respective proper officers thereunto duly authorized.

3. Defendant, having been interrupted *in flagrante delicto*, can hardly be heard to assert that his conduct was not the *causa causans* of the injury.

4. NOW THEREFORE, BE IT KNOWN that in consideration of the premises as well as in consideration of the sum of Five Thousand Dollars ($5,000.00) paid in hand by Licensee to Licensor contemporaneously with the delivery by Licensor to Licensee of a duly executed copy of this License Agreement, and in consideration of the royalty payments herein specified to be paid by Licensee to Licensor, and in consideration of the terms, conditions, and covenants herein set forth, it is mutually agreed and covenanted by and between Licensor and Licensee as follows, to wit:

5. It is my desire and intention to give and provide to my beloved stepdaughter, the said Angelina, a full and complete education, including post-graduate training if that be her interest, wish and desire. I do therefore hereby give, devise, and bequeath unto her, to have and to hold, all my right, title, and interest in and to the following properties described hereinbelow.

6. *Hazard or Property Insurance* Borrower shall keep the improvements now existing or hereafter erected on the Property insured against loss by fire, hazards

included within the term "extended coverage" and any other hazards, including floods or flooding, for which Lender requires insurance. This insurance shall be maintained in the amounts and for the periods that Lender requires. The insurance carrier providing the insurance shall be chosen by Borrower subject to Lender's approval which shall not be unreasonably withheld. If Borrower fails to maintain coverage described above, Lender may, at Lender's option, obtain coverage to protect Lender's rights in the Property in accordance with paragraph 17.

7. If the funds held by Lender in the Impound Account exceed the amounts permitted to be held by applicable law, Lender shall account to Borrower for the excess funds in accordance with the requirements of applicable law. If the amount of the funds held by Lender in the Impound Account at any time is not sufficient to pay the Escrow Items when due, Lender may so notify Borrower in writing, and, in such case, Borrower shall pay to Lender the amount necessary to make up the deficiency. Borrower shall make up the deficiency in no more than twelve monthly payments, at Lender's sole discretion.

8. The beneficiary or trustee named in a deed of trust or mortgagee named in a mortgage with power of sale upon real property or any interest therein to secure a debt or other obligation, or if there be a successor or successors in interest, then such successor or successors in interest, shall have the right to bring suit to foreclose the same in the manner and subject to the provisions, rights and remedies relating to the foreclosure of a mortgage upon such property.

❧ Exercise 16A

When you rewrite the following passages, pay special attention to your choice of words.

1. Every person who shall unlawfully throw out a switch, remove a rail, or place any obstruction on any railroad with the intention of derailing any passenger, freight, or other train, car, or engine, or who shall unlawfully place any dynamite or other explosive material or any other obstruction upon or near the track of any railroad with the intention of blowing up or derailing any such train, car, or engine, or who shall unlawfully set fire to any railroad bridge or trestle, over which any such train, car, or engine must pass, with the intention of wrecking such train, car, or engine, shall be guilty of a felony, and shall be punished by imprisonment in the state prison for life without possibility of parole.

2. Advertisers are hereby notified that it is the policy of this newspaper to refuse publication of any material designed for the purpose of encouraging, promoting, influencing, or advancing the sale of any products, wares, goods, commodities, services, or the like, which because of its content, form, style, substance, appearance, or manner of presentation is or may be likely to cause any reader thereof to believe that said material is an article, story, column, editorial, or similar nonadvertising portion of this newspaper.

3. Attorney's Fee. In all cases of foreclosure of mortgage the attorney's fee shall be fixed by the court in which the proceedings are had, any stipulation in the mortgage to the contrary notwithstanding.

4. **Stay or Injunction Pending Appeal**
Stay Must Ordinarily Be Sought in the First Instance in District Court
Application for a stay of the judgment or order of a district court pending appeal, or for approval of a supersedeas bond, or for an order suspending, modifying, restoring, or granting an injunction during the pendency of an appeal must ordinarily be made in the first instance in the district court. [Fed. R. App. P. 8(a) (1997).]

❧ Exercise 17A

1. Rewrite this passage to eliminate the elegant variation:

   An attorney is subject to professional discipline for incompetence. Proceedings to impose professional sanction may be commenced against practitioners who undertake matters they know they are not sufficiently skilled to handle. Further, lawyers who accept a case and then fail to prepare to handle the matter in an able manner can be censured, suspended, or disbarred. Not only attorney discipline but also civil liability for malpractice must be taken into consideration. In actions for professional negligence, lawyers can be held liable for damages proximately caused by their incompetence. Plaintiffs in legal malpractice litigation include not only clients, but also other persons who were intended to benefit from the services rendered by the defendant practitioner.

2. Eliminate the multiple negatives in this passage:

   It shall be a violation of these rules for any member to fail to post a notice in a prominent place that is not obscured from public view listing the member's retail prices for all items offered for sale, excepting only limited time special sale prices offered for not more than three days.

3. The following passage is from a bulletin written by an in-house lawyer for a corporation. The purpose of the bulletin is to inform the corporation's employees about a new legal service plan. When you rewrite the passage, avoid cosmic detachment by addressing it directly to the employees, and make the passage as simple and easy to read as you can:

Entitlement to participation in the Employee Legal Service Plan is dependent upon the employee's compliance with the following requirements: (a) employment with the company must have commenced at least thirty (30) days prior to enrollment by the employee in the Plan; (b) employment must be on a Regular Staff basis, the Plan not being available to any person employed on either a Casual or Temporary Help basis; and (c) the employee must have submitted a completed Employee Legal Service Plan Enrollment Form to Personnel & Employment Services, and an appropriate Payroll Deduction Request must have been filed by the employee with Accounting & Payroll.

4. The following passage is from a book intended for lawyers who wish to work on the legal staff of a corporation. Revise it to eliminate the sexist language:

The function of in-house corporate counsel in administering litigation is sometimes said to be limited: his job is to achieve the best practical results at the lowest reasonable cost. He has done his work well if he selects the best man as outside trial counsel, and then reviews the matter from time to time to make sure things are proceeding on course. That view is unsound for many reasons. The trial lawyer is an important link between the corporation and the public; frequently he is called on to respond in the heat of battle with little or no notice. Generally his interests and perceptions are far different from the corporate executive, the man who lives daily within the corporation. The outside trial lawyer may be an expert in trial strategy, tactics, and practice, but he is almost certainly no expert in corporate management and policy. In-house corporate counsel need not have had trial experience to manage litigation, though it helps if he has earned his spurs in a few years of law firm practice. But it is important that he know enough about litigation to handle policy decisions, judge the effectiveness of trial counsel, and administer those matters which are his primary responsibility.

5. The following passage about the attorney-client privilege has too much elegant variation, too many nominalizations, too much passive voice, and too many unnecessary words. Revise it.

   Provision has been made in every American jurisdiction—in some instances by statute, in other instances by evidence code, and in still other situations by judge-made decisional law—that, generally speaking, no requirement can be imposed upon a client or upon a legal practitioner respecting revelation, by way of testimony or otherwise, of communications theretofore transmitted in confidence between the lay person and the professional in the course of requests for or provision of legal advice or other types of legal services.

6. Revise this negative passage to make it as positive as you can:

   "Dependent relative" includes a member's child or adopted child who has not attained the age of 18 or has not ceased to receive full-time education or training. [Martin Cutts, The Plain English Guide 68 (1995).]

7. Revise the following passage to make it less verbose and more gender neutral:

Decline due to increased age provides an explanation for the fact that when an academic or professional gets older, he has a tendency not to keep up with the literature in his field as assiduously as younger men do. Absorption of new information is relatively higher in cost to the older man than to the younger, because of the erosion of the older man's fluid intelligence, and additionally there is a decline in the amount of benefit; for the older man it is relatively smaller as a consequence of having fewer periods remaining during which a return can be earned on whatever new human capital he has acquired.

8. Rid this passage of its cosmic detachment and stuffy tone:

The risks of injury sought to be eliminated by this Consumer Product Safety Commission standard are lacerations, contusions, abrasions, and other injuries or death resulting from walking or running into glazed doors or sliding glass doors believed to be open, or glazed panels mistaken as a means of ingress or egress, or falling into or through glazed doors, sliding glass doors, glazed panels, bathtub doors and enclosures and shower doors and enclosures.

❧ Exercise 18A

1. Some of the following sentences contain acceptable punctuation, and others contain punctuation errors. Fix the punctuation errors, but never mind the abysmal writing style.

(a) No article of wearing apparel subject to the Act shall be marketed if: such article when tested according to the procedures prescribed below is so highly-flammable as to be dangerous when worn by individuals.

(b) To compute the average time of flame-spread for each set of wearing apparel specimens at least two of the specimens' must ignite and burn the stop cord for the specimen.

(c) However if fewer than two specimens of any given set of five ignite, and burn the entire length of the specimen the test results shall be interpreted according to subparagraphs 1–4; below.

(d) If no specimen ignites and burns the stop cord the results of that test shall be regarded as Class 1 (passing.)

(e) If only one of five specimens of a plain surface fabric ignites—and burns the stop cord with a time of 3.5 seconds or more: the results of that test shall be regarded as Class 1 (passing).

(f) If only one of five specimens of a raised-fiber surface fabric ignites and burns in less than four seconds but the base fabric does not "ignite or fuse, the results of that test shall be regarded as Class 1 passing.

2. Repunctuate the following passage, breaking apart sentences where necessary, repairing incomplete sentences, and making other punctuation changes as needed.

The paradigmatic early-twentieth-century case was *Lochner v. New York*, the opposing opinions there were written by Justices Peckham and Holmes the polar opposites of the jurisprudence of the day. *Lochner* itself now stands near the top of any list of discredited Supreme Court decisions and when commentators discuss the case at all they use it to illustrate the drastic change in jurisprudence during the twentieth-century which has seen the Holmes' dissent elevated to established doctrine. Joseph Lochner had been convicted for violating a New York law by requiring a worker in his bakery to work more than sixty hours in one week. The law was challenged as a violation of due process an unreasonable exercise of the police power. The Justices first voted by a bare majority to uphold the law and the case was assigned to Justice Harlan who wrote a draft opinion for the Court. Justice Peckham writing a strong draft dissent. Before the case came down however there was a vote switch the Peckham dissent became the opinion of the Court; and the Harlan opinion a dissent. The changed vote was probably Justice Fullers'. Earlier cases that upheld work-hour regulations were regarded as health measures. In *Lochner*, Justice McKenna who's father had owned a bakery may have convinced Fuller and others in the majority that bakery work was not dangerous; and that the health rationale was a sham.

3. Correct the punctuation and make whatever other revisions you think are needed in the following passage:

When a lawyer serves the government for a period, and then leaves to enter private law practice the government has a right to expect that it's confidential information will not be abused. Further private clients should not be allowed to gain unfair advantage from information known to a lawyer only because of his' or her' prior government service and lawyers should not be in a position to benefit private clients because of prior, government service. Finally; possible future benefit to private clients should not distort a lawyers' professional judgment while working for the government. All of the foregoing would suggest: that there should be a broad rigid rule of disqualification, for lawyers who move from the government to private practice! Such a rule however would have a serious draw-back, the government would be hindered in recruiting good lawyers for short-term government service. Thus—the A.B.A Model Code of Professional Responsibility ('ABA Code,') and the A.B.A Model Rule's of Professional Conduct ("A.B.A. Model Rules) strike a compromise by establishing disqualification rules, that are relatively narrow, and flexible. Except when expressly permitted by law a lawyer who leaves government service, and enters private law practice must not represent a private client in a, "...matter..." in which the lawyer participated: "...personally and substantially—" while in government service (unless the government agency consents after consultation. That raises a question about "matters'" meaning? As used in the rule the term 'matter...' does not mean: "a general topic", or "broad subject area". Rather it means a specific set of facts, involving specific parties. A.B.A Model Rule 1.11(d) defines, "matter," more fully as: "any judicial or other proceeding, application or request for a ruling or other determination; contract, claim, controversy, investigation charge, accusation arrest or other particular matter involving a specific party or parties."

Index and Lawyer's Word Guide